THE MILLENNIUM BUG

Is this the end of the world as we know it?

JON PAULIEN

Pacific Press® Publishing Association
Nampa, Idaho
Oshawa, Ontario, Canada

Edited by B. Russell Holt
Cover and inside art direction and design: Michelle C. Petz
    Mechanical insect: Marcus M. Mashburn
    Earth: © 1999 Photodisc, Inc.
    Clock: Michelle C. Petz

ISBN 0-8163-1755-0

Contents

Foreword

This book brings us face to face with the questions whirling about what it means to come to the end of one thousand-year period and the beginning of another. It pulls no punches. Dr. Jon Paulien, professor of New Testament interpretation at the Andrews University Seventh-day Adventist Theological Seminary and recognized internationally as one of the leading specialists on the book of Revelation, is no newcomer to this subject. He already has published another book in this field.

But *The Millennium Bug: Is This the End of the World as We Know It?* carries us right to the point in a fast-moving, readable explanation that answers dozens of questions. Not only is the book attention-catching, it is based on solid, biblical research presented in a non-technical, easy-to-understand style.

How did such a book come to be? Sensing the need for a clear, reliable discussion of the coming millennial landmark, the Biblical Research Institute of the General Conference of Seventh-day Adventists asked Dr. Paulien to do the necessary research and to prepare a book answering the questions surrounding the year 2000. It is with genuine satisfaction that the Biblical Research Institute Committee commends *The Millennium Bug* to a wide reading public, not the least of whom will be Seventh-day Adventists who eagerly look forward to Jesus' soon return.

George W. Reid, Th.D., Director
Biblical Research Institute
Silver Spring, Maryland
March 1999

Introduction

It didn't take a genius to anticipate the excitement surrounding the year 2000. In the summer of 1987 at a camp meeting in Lincoln, Nebraska, I joked that the worst imaginable job would be to teach about end-time events at the Seminary in the years leading up to the year 2000. I suggested then that the natural Adventist interest in the events leading up to the end of the world would be compounded by a corresponding interest in the secular world. I foresaw the danger that wild-eyed speculation might replace sober attention to what the Bible has to say about the end of the world.

About five years ago I sought to address this issue with the book *What the Bible Says About the End-Time*, published by the Review and Herald Publishing Association. In that book I tried to lay out the broad biblical perspective on the final events of earth's history and their timing. That book has recently been reprinted in paperback, so I decided not to repeat the contents of that book here.

More recently, the Biblical Research Institute Committee of the General Conference of Seventh-day Adventists asked me to write a book that would focus on the current situation in the world as we approach the end of the calendrical millennium. The committee felt that the Adventist people needed specific guidance in the face of the millennial call to excitement. Concerns were raised about how to keep a balance between a healthy Adventist expectation of the End and healthy attention to the ongoing concerns of life in this world. Given the sobering yet real possibility that God will permit history and human existence on this planet to continue beyond the year 2000, how does God want us to live? While the committee gave considerable input and found itself in general agreement with the final product, I, as the author, must take responsibility for its shortcomings.

In this book I turn my attention to some of the latest headlines in order to apply that biblical perspective to the events that the world is facing in our day. I have sought to maintain a steady head and a long-range perspective in the midst of fascinating events that may or may not prove to be of eternal significance. Even as I write I feel the pull of excitement as report after report, movie after movie, and technological advance after technological advance all seem to indicate that we are living in unprecedented times. In the midst of it all, I have tried to keep the biblical perspective constantly before me.

Truly momentous events *are* happening in the world. How to relate to them is the problem we face. On the one hand, we don't want to ignore genuine evidences of the End and find ourselves unprepared when it happens. On the other hand, we don't want to replay the excesses of the past. Finding our balance between the two extremes is uniquely challenging in today's world.

I pray that, as you hear more and more about rocks hurtling through space in our direction, this book will help to keep you anchored to The Rock. I pray that as the Internet multiplies the dissemination of words about the End, that this book will help to keep you solid in The Word. I pray that as many voices call you to follow a variety of paths, this book will help to keep you close to Him who is The Way.

CHAPTER 1

Y2K: The Year 2000 Surprise

THE DAY ARRIVES

It's the morning of January 1, A.D. 2000. It is surprisingly light out. You snap out of sleep mode to check the digital clock over the headboard of your bed. It is blank. "Stupid clock!" you say to yourself, "It never works when you need it." You reach over to turn on the bedside lamp. It's not working either. Suddenly you realize that the alarm clock is not the problem. The power is out.

You get up and grab a robe from the closet. The chill in the air leads you to exchange that robe for a warmer one. You head out to the living room to check the battery-operated wall clock. It's 8:37 a.m. Good thing you don't have to go to work today. "My but it's cold in here," you start thinking, "The power must have been off for some time." You immediately think of the food in the refrigerator, comforted to know you can move a lot of it out onto the deck, if necessary, where the cold and the snow can preserve it.

"I wonder how many homes are affected by this blackout," you think, "maybe I should call the electric company and make sure they know about this." So you open the drawer in the kitchen where you keep the phone book, look up the emergency number for the electric utility and pick up the receiver. Something is not right. In a few seconds you realize that your uneasy feeling stems from the absence of a dial tone, or of any sound at all. Then you remember that your cordless phone is dependent on electricity from an outlet in order to function. You put down the receiver and head for your mobile, battery-operated phone. It's working, but it flashes a constant "out of range" message.

You feel the first twinge of panic in your lower intestine. There is something seriously wrong here! Grabbing a portable radio you head for the fireplace to start building a fire while you turn on the all-news station to see if you can learn anything about the situation. Instead of news you get what sounds like a talk show. You check around the dial, but your news station seems nowhere to be found. You finally realize that the "talk show" *is* the news.

The electricity is off at the station as well, but they are continuing to broadcast with a backup, gasoline-fired generator. The problem is, there isn't much news, so the reporters are sitting around speculating about the situation more than reporting hard facts. Why? Without electricity and working phone lines their access to the usual news sources is intermittent at best. And even when they achieve access, they discover that the news-gathering organizations themselves are having difficulty getting news! So apparently the problems you are having are quite widespread![1] This is brought home with devastating force when you head down to your hardware superstore a couple of days later to buy a back-up generator to provide electricity for your house. The associate who waits on you just shakes his head and says, "Where have you been recently? Generators have been out of stock for two months now, and in the last three days we've received orders that will take five months to fill![2] Would you like to get on the waiting list?"

THE STORY UNFOLDS

Over the next several days you battle darkness, cold, and food spoilage while gradually piecing together details about the enormous catastrophe that has just struck the world. You learn that the world has caught the millennium bug, sometimes known as the Y2K problem (Y2K is an acronym for the year 2000). You suddenly remember that Y2K was the title of a blockbuster, summer of 1999, disaster movie that you didn't take very seriously.

You discover that the year 2000 problem is both trivial and overwhelming at the same time.[3] In short, the millennium bug goes back to the beginnings of computing in the 60s, 70s and 80s.[4] Computer designers wrote software and programmed chips and computer time clocks that recorded years with only the last two digits, 75 instead of 1975, for example. They chose this method primarily to conserve computer memory (of all the short-sighted decisions!).

Unfortunately, these programs record the year 2000 as "00" which a computer interprets as "1900." Now this may seem minor to most people. The problem, however, is that most computer software programs are quite fragile. A single bug in the program can cause it to seize up or crash.[5] As a result, older mainframe computers, along with many PCs and software programs either crashed or started providing false information on January 1, 2000.

The solution to the problem had also seemed trivial. The two-digit date fields could be found and replaced with four-digit ones. Software programs could be "trained" to recognize future years from 0 to whatever as being in the twenty-first century. New software programs could be written to replace older ones that were too difficult to fix. But two complications combined to derail all of those solutions.

First there was the problem of time. Business, governments, and organizations became aware of the problem fairly late into the 90s. By then two-digit date fields had been embedded in billions and billions of lines of software code (1998 estimates ran from 180 billion to 700 billion).[6] And not only were there hundreds of millions of computers in the world to deal with, there were probably hundreds of billions of tiny "computers" embedded in the form of chips in appliances, elevators, security systems, manufacturing plants, and medical devices like heart monitors and CAT scanners.[7] Millions of computer techies putting in thousands of hours each were needed to go over all the codes and ensure Y2K compliance in every computer, program, device, and operation. As events unfolded there just weren't enough skilled people around to do the job in the time that was left. And testing the "fixed" systems turned out to be even more time-consuming than repairing the noncompliant code.

The second, and in the end fatal, complication was that the majority of all software programs were part of a bigger corporate, industrial, educational, and governmental network that has become truly global in its reach. Each system in the network depends on information provided by other systems and other programs throughout the network. Unless all systems in the network could be made Y2K compliant, no system would be totally safe on the fateful date.[8] If a single bug can bring down a software program, imagine the impact of hundreds, thousands, even millions of bugs cascading over the net all at once![9]

Most American and many European corporations went out of their way to be ready for Y2K and generally succeeded internally. But it was not enough. Things that worked well when tested within a corporation often didn't work when they were linked together with others in the system on the night of January 1. Compliant companies found that even when their systems linked up with other companies that had solved their Y2K problems, the varying strategies they had used to solve their problems sometimes resulted in fatal incompatibilities when the new year came.[10] Incompatibilities from one system to the next triggered problems in still others and the whole thing snowballed into a massive network shutdown that disabled the majority of vital services worldwide.

It also became clear that the network was more affected than anyone had realized by the quality of systems in emerging countries.[11] Many corporations in the United States and Europe had used the prospect of high salaries to lure computer technicians away from emerging countries over the last four years of the millennium.[12] But problems in those same countries were now bringing much of the system down, compliant going down with noncompliant.[13]

In 1998, many computer technicians "saw the handwriting on the wall" and began talking about TEOTWAWKI, "The End Of The World As We Know It."[14] Some of them began abandoning the urban lifestyle and its amenities and staking out well-stocked and well-defended hideouts in remote areas. Almost overnight sober-headed "computer geeks" became "survivalists."[15] Fortunately, by the middle of 1999 most communities in North America announced the cancellation of all vacations for police and other emergency personnel from December, 1999 through March of 2000, so social disruptions have turned out to be minimal.[16] The city of Toronto in Canada even went so far as to insist that all 5000 police officers be on duty daily from December 27 through January 9. Vancouver has extended that policy to January 14.[17] Hospital and electric company workers were denied vacations throughout the months of December and January.[18] Having key people "on duty" when the millennium turned went a long way to minimize what might otherwise have been catastrophic disruptions. The next best thing to being compliant in advance was to have "SWAT teams" in place to deal with emergencies as they happened.

A corresponding blessing was the decision in the U.S. Congress to make January 3-5, 2000 a "Y2K holiday."[19] This meant that all nonessential employees were required to stay home until January 6, to give information technology people the chance to stress-test their systems and bring them online slowly, a piece at a time, rather than under peak load conditions. As weak links appeared, personnel were in place to repair items quickly or just take them "off-line" until there would be sufficient time and personnel to fix them properly. By January 6 everybody knew what was working and what was not in their little part of the world.

POWER GOES OUT

Over the next several days you keep listening to the radio and slowly learn the full extent of the problem. On January 1, 53 percent of the homes and businesses in North America and Western Europe, and 78 percent of those in the rest of the world were deprived of electricity.[20] Indications are that it will be weeks before all of the developed world has its power back, and months (possibly years in some cases) before the developing world is back on line. The best piece of news in all this is that the safety-related devices on nuclear reactors do not rely on date-driven databases in order to function. As a result, with one exception (a couple of small, older reactors in the hinterlands of Kazakhstan) there have been no serious nuclear safety problems. On the other hand, the basic systems necessary for plant operations[21] turned out to be more date sensitive than regulators had anticipated. So even though safety was not an issue, most nuclear plants were off line until the computer glitches could be fixed. In some parts of Europe this idled as much as 70 percent of generating capacity.[22]

Coal, gas, and oil-fired electric plants themselves proved far less dependent on computer systems. But glitches in the computers that manage the transportation system resulted in reduced deliveries of coal, gas, and oil after the first of the year. Gas-fired plants had the most problems, at first, since gas is generally supplied on a just-in-time basis. Rescue by coal and oil-fired plants didn't materialize either. Due to the ongoing effect of rail company mergers in 1997 and the unusually severe weather in the final quarter of 1999, coal and oil stockpiles were fairly low at the beginning of the year. There was, therefore, no way to compensate for the 17 percent loss of power that occurred with the shutdown of most nuclear reactors on the first of January. And a couple of weeks later some of the coal and oil-fired plants ran out of fuel, further delaying the reestablishment of power to many areas.[23]

To make things even worse, electric power is controlled and delivered by massive, continent-wide grids. The 17 percent loss in electric production caused overloaded grid-control computers (some of which had also gone down) to play triage with the power supply to whole regions, resulting in blackouts far out of proportion to the actual loss of power.[24] But after a week or so, a federal takeover of the power grid and the allocation of resources led the way to getting a handle on the problem. It was determined that a carefully planned system of power rotation and rationing could alleviate much of the suffering related to heating and electrical problems. Food spoilage, however, remains a major issue.

The rotation system, however, was not an equal one. Smaller regional utilities had far greater Y2K problems than the major utilities around the country. To protect the major centers of population, the operators of the electric grid cut off many struggling rural operations from the general electrical supply. A delicious irony (to some) is the fact that remote areas of the country remained dark for weeks and even months after the first of the year. This left thousands of Y2K "survivalists" waiting in their isolated cabins for the lights to come back on in their neighborhoods while the "clueless" urban dwellers enjoyed relatively uninterrupted service.[25]

TELECOMMUNICATIONS

You also learn about another devastating problem, the breakdown of many tele-communications networks. While most of the major telephone companies in the United States turned out to be Y2K compliant there were still serious problems in 20-25 percent of the country.[26] With that much of the country largely off-line, thousands of deaths have occurred because sick and elderly people, trapped in homes without heat or power, were unable to contact emergency services. Numerous other agencies, such as the National Weather Service, the Blood Service of the American Red Cross, and the United Network for Organ Sharing have been strongly handicapped by the disruptions in telephone service.[27]

The situation is far worse in other parts of the world. Asian nations, distracted by the financial crisis of 1997-1999, were far less ready for the year 2000 than North America. East Asia, therefore, joined the underdeveloped nations in suffering huge disruptions in telecommunications services as the year 2000 dawned. The communications failures in some countries had an immediate impact on international trade and investment. Major long-distance phone companies began refusing to connect calls to non-compliant countries.[28] A shortage of Asian parts soon resulted in the shutdown of manufacturing plants throughout the world.[29] The effect on the U.S. and European economies might soon become nearly as great as it already is elsewhere.

Perhaps the ultimate irony is this. The infrastructure of the Internet was designed to withstand a nuclear attack, but was helpless in the face of people's inability to get a dial tone! But there is some good news here after all. As phone service returned, it became evident that the vast network of routers and gateways, hubs and switches, provides multiple pathways between points. This allows messages and information to bypass noncompliant segments and remain available with, at most, a few slowdowns in response.[30]

TRAVEL

You also learn that air travel has been seriously curtailed. Scores of older mainframe computers at air traffic control centers around the world shut down on January 1. The backbone of the air traffic control system in the United States has been 225 mainframe computers, including 71 purchased in the early 1980s and discontinued by the manufacturer around 1988.[31] When fixing a number of them was finally deemed impossible in early 1999, attempts to get enough replacements on line before the deadline proved to be futile. Contingency planning for those areas was left to paper, pencils, binoculars, and the equivalent of ham radio, with predictable results when the new year came around. The breakdown was nearly total in some parts of Africa and the former Soviet Union. As a result, whole countries have become "no-fly zones" ever since; in individual cases this may last for months.[32]

Problems were not limited to air traffic control. Major safety concerns caused six major overseas airlines to shut down entirely when Lloyd's of London declared them "uninsurable." All airlines have been affected to some degree. Secret testing back in 1999 determined that embedded microchips in aircraft electronic equipment raised safety questions with regard to all air fleets. That resulted in the large-scale grounding of most airplanes built before 1993, the largest part of the air fleet, when the new year began. A month into the new millennium air traffic worldwide is functioning at about 57 percent of 1999 levels and is gradually increasing. This is proving to be less of a problem than expected, since fear of accidents and problems at home made passenger demand far less than it would normally have been.[33]

Meanwhile, back on the ground, embedded chips are also creating problems in passenger cars, trucks, and buses. Cars and trucks from the 1997 model-year on are year 2000 compliant. Few cars built before the mid-80s had computers at all. The vehicles in between, however, are running into a variety of unusual difficulties, from not starting at all to problems with timing, fuel delivery, and false diagnoses of maintenance problems. Some bus companies have been forced to reduce schedules to make up for the increased vehicle down time, just at a time when a lot of people are seeing buses as a safe alternative to flying. An interesting side effect is that in warmer parts of the world, bicycles are now in short supply. Older cars and trucks are also harder and harder to find, sending the prices of "junkers" to unheard-of levels.

MONEY PROBLEMS

By mid-1999 banks had already begun to stop lending to corporations that they believed would not be ready in time for the year 2000. Toward the end of 1999, they also declared a worldwide seven-day banking holiday for the beginning of the new year. The cumulative effect of these two actions nearly caused a panic. Millions of bank customers around the world tried to withdraw large sums at the end of December, not only to cover for the next week, but also in case the bank's computers lost track of their money. The brief panic largely subsided when banks and brokerage houses assured their customers that the last paper statements of 1999 would be considered the legal basis for all accounts when the new year hit.[34] After the first of the year, the Federal Reserve backed up the banks with more than two-hundred fifty billion dollars in short-term loans.[35] Short-term interest rates also shot up as an incentive to keep savings in the system.

But continuing problems in the worldwide telecommunications net caused bank transfers over phone lines to grind virtually to a halt in that second week.[36] Worse yet, even when banks themselves were Y2K compliant, computer-corrupted data from noncompliant banks created a spiraling crescendo of unintentional misinformation.[37] As a result, many bankers quickly discovered that they could no longer trust their general ledgers or the account balances of their customers. Even the Federal Reserve Bank has switched to a paper-based payment and record system for the immediate future, keeping many workers on duty seven days a week.[38] While paper records provide the security of being able to set things right eventually, computer-based errors quickly led to financial nightmares that will keep accountants and auditors busy for months and possibly even years to come.[39]

Notwithstanding the banking problems in North America, the situation is far worse in Europe and Japan. The Europeans spent most of 1999 distracted by the changeover to a common currency, the Euro, a process that cost three to four times as much as the efforts put in to solve the year 2000 problem.[40] Eleven countries were operating two currencies at the end of 1999, a situation that would have been nightmarish enough by itself, if the year 2000 hadn't come along. This caused the problems related to computer misinformation and the switch to paper accounting to be multiplied four-fold over the situation in North America. Things are little better in Japan, where the wrenching financial deregulation of 1998-1999 forced Japanese banks to learn a whole new way of doing business, only to be confronted by the mother of all banking problems. Smaller companies in Japan, on the other hand, are having an even worse time because the credit crunch of the previous couple of years prevented them from raising sufficient cash to deal with the problem.

GOVERNMENT

You gradually learn that the crisis has affected government even more than areas controlled largely by private business. The Financial Management Service of the Treasury Department, which writes and mails many of the checks sent by government, failed to be ready on time. Anticipating this problem, Congress voted in October of 1999 to shift significant responsibility for all retirement and disability benefit checks from the Treasury Department to the Social Security Administration, which was already fully compliant.[41] So retirees got their checks in January and February as fast as the transportation system allowed. But a nasty trap was sprung when 42 of the 54 state operations that handle disability payments for Social Security (the Disability Determination Services system) crashed, leaving the disability system in shambles.

The Department of Defense is also in serious disarray, along with its counterparts among the major powers of the world. U.S. officials are in continuing contact with defense leaders in NATO, Russia, China, and other nations with nuclear capability. The big concern is the possibility of accidental launches and false alarms related to their nuclear weapons arsenals. Exchanges of personnel were made in December, 1999, to ensure trust and clear communication.[42] The year 1999 also saw numerous "back channel" contacts with nations who denied their nuclear capability or were hostile to the United States.[43] Oddly enough, where military computers fail to turn on at all, the danger is minimal. But where computers are operating with unreliable data, the danger is enormous, requiring live human backups to ensure reliability.

Further problems are plaguing the defense community. The Global Command and Control system is functioning but in an erratic manner, making it difficult for commanders to plan, execute, and manage military operations. As a result of the latter, the Defense Department was severely hampered in responding to a series of terrorist actions which took advantage of Y2K confusion in early January. Malicious programmers funded by a hostile nation, probably in the Middle East or Asia, managed to hack their way into the CIA and National Security Agency, adding to the confusion. Fortunately, it seems not to have occurred yet to some of the world's "rogue states" that the loss of computer guidance provides the great equalizer in any Gulf War type challenge to U.S. power.[44]

There is an ironic piece of good news in all of this governmental confusion. The least compliant of all governmental entities in the United States turned out to be the Internal Revenue Service. Modernization decisions made in the mid-1980s and implemented in 1988 made things worse rather than better with regard to the year 2000 changeover. Reductions in personnel combined with massive changes in the tax code in 1997 made Y2K compliance impossible. The coming of the new year resulted in a flood of erroneous tax notices, groundless bills, and refunds with figures sometimes into the millions. On January 24, Congress virtually shut down the IRS, suspending all audits for the foreseeable future and invalidating all messages sent since January 1. The American people were instructed to suspend all work on their 1999 tax forms and continue withholding and sending in quarterly payments at previous rates. There is talk of instituting a simple flat tax system to handle 1999 returns, and implementing a national sales tax for 2000 and beyond. In the end, taxes continue to flow, but some of the hassles and audit abuse may become a thing of the past.

THE SNOWBALL EFFECT

As January moves into February and March, life is returning to more normal conditions in the United States. A number of secondary consequences of the Y2K problem begin to sink in, however, as you continue to gather information about the crisis. In a special sense, the year 2000 problem came at an unusually bad time in world history. In the 1970s oil was the basic source of the energy that ran the world's economy. But today the key fuel of the world economy is information. And the world is more dependent on information now than it was on oil before.

By February companies who had tried to hide their year 2000 problems started being hit by lawsuits resulting from costs related to products and services that were not Y2K compliant.[45] Auto manufacturers tried to forestall such suits in January by offering massive recalls on most models from the years 1988-1997. But consumers are not appeased by this action since auto repair shops are booking as much as three months in advance. Costs related to the Y2K problem have already caused two smaller auto companies to declare bankruptcy. The remaining companies are involved in a flurry of strategic merger talks in the hopes of salvaging venerable nameplates. It is expected that by mid-year there will only be six mega-companies left in the automobile world, two each based in Japan, the United States, and Germany.

Computer companies are in even more trouble. Lawsuits pushed a major maker of main-frame computers into bankruptcy the first week of February, along with the biggest name in personal computers. Mainframes built before 1990 are still the mainstay of many operations, yet have proven in many cases to be unfixable. Few personal computers built before mid-1997 have turned out to be year 2000 compliant, and many of these are not upgradeable.

No one knows how many lawsuits may develop over the next few years as a result of the failure of radios used by police, fire, ambulance, and other emergency services. The chips embedded in many of these systems were too old to upgrade, and by the time communities became aware of the problem, it was too late to supply them all with new equipment.

Several marginal department and chain stores went under when an avalanche of defective product returns pushed their negative cash flows after Christmas over the brink. Others stores are expected to follow them as the lawsuits begin to hit because products they sell cause damage to property, life, and health. But in Asia, things are far worse. From 1997-1999 Asian companies were so concerned about avoiding bankruptcy during the currency meltdown that Y2K was put on the back burner until it was too late. In the Pacific Rim, therefore, nearly 45 percent of companies have either declared bankruptcy or are desperately exploring merger options in order to survive in some form. The one area of exception is Japan, where a tradition of lifetime employment in larger companies meant that the same people who wrote the software were usually still around to debug it. This is making Japan's Y2K problem easier to fix than in most other Asian countries.

Problems in developing countries led to problems in North America as well. Since the plastics used in food packaging are largely manufactured in developing countries, serious shortages in the manufacture and delivery of plastics for packaging are resulting in spot shortages of many processed foods even in Europe and North America.[46] Many people are being forced to change their dietary habits as well as their lifestyles. And computer prices are rising for the first time in memory as just-in-time manufacturing collapses in the wake of Asia's devastation. Manufacturing, testing, and shipping of Asian-made computer hardware have been deeply affected by the millennium bug.[47]

The problem of embedded chips is taking a peculiar twist. It seemed at first that fewer embedded chips were date-sensitive than was previously thought. There were surprisingly few immediate disruptions when January 1 came around. But a nasty surprise is turning up. Many embedded systems work by intervals, rather than specific dates. Items on thirty, sixty, or hundred-day cycles are shutting down suddenly and at seemingly random intervals well after the first of January. So just as the world is getting a handle on systemic problems, individual traffic lights, cars, elevators, mobile phones, copy machines, ATMs, pacemakers, and power grid relays are shutting down, seemingly at random. Even in February of 2000 it is clear that new dimensions of the date change problem are going to keep turning up for some time yet.

Thankfully, your phone service has returned at last, and along with it, your access to the Internet. But there was a price. As the world became more and more aware of the problem of interconnectivity, the more compliant nations began cutting connections with parts of Asia, Africa, South America, and Europe.[48] Reasonably healthy nations quarantined the

"Internet lepers" whose non-compliant code contaminated the whole system. As noted earlier, major phone companies are refusing to place or accept calls from countries that have not brought their telecommunications systems into compliance.[49]

Nations like the United States, the Netherlands, and Australia are becoming islands of recovery, placing national survival over worldwide cooperation. An International Computer Technology Fund (modeled on the International Monetary Fund) has been set up to assist nations willing to pay the price to get their computer networks back up to speed. In exchange, those nations will have to pass rigorous tests based on high standards in order to regain access to the system.

IS THIS FOR REAL?

Is the above scenario really possible? It is certainly a worst-case type of scenario, but hard evidence as I write indicates that not one single aspect of the account is totally impossible.[50] The bottom line is that the full effect of the date change on the worldwide network of computers is untestable in advance. It would be impossible to get all computers in the world set to a future date at the same time. That means that no one can predict ahead of time exactly what will happen when the clock strikes midnight at the turn of the millennium. As I write, American intelligence agencies, according to *U.S. News and World Report*,[51] are entertaining three options concerning the Y2K bug, (1) brownout, with a brief loss of power; (2) blackout, when virtually the entire country goes dark but quickly recovers; and (3) total meltdown, with rioting, looting, and social unrest in urban areas. The scenario of this chapter is closest to number two.

While it never took a genius to figure out that the year 2000 would attract a huge amount of attention when it arrived, no one expected the date itself to carry such fateful significance. Is it any wonder that many Bible believers are asking whether the possibility of events like these might portend the opening salvo of the final events portrayed in the Bible?[52]

Actually, one aspect of the above scenario is extremely unlikely. By the middle of 1999, books like this and the summer disaster movie *Y2K* will have alerted the average citizen to the problem. There will also be advance warning as to the severity of the problem because of related glitches that may strike already in 1999.[53] So it is quite unlikely that most people will be surprised if there are unusual problems when the millennium arrives. In fact, widespread advance knowledge about the problem implies that panic conditions in banking and the stock market, should they occur, might well precede the year 2000 by many months.[54]

As I write, governments, corporations, and small businesses are beginning to throw billions of dollars at the year 2000 problem.[55] U.S. governmental agencies are showing increasing optimism as the fateful date approaches.[56] Based on my wide-ranging research, I am optimistic that the overall picture will not be nearly as bad as the scenario I have portrayed here. But I also consider it likely that at least some aspects of the scenario will in fact occur. And it is impossible to say in advance just which systems are most likely to break down.[57] To me it is unrealistic, therefore, to expect that the date will pass without considerable disruption in many parts of the world.[58]

Whatever actually happens on January 1, 2000, Bible believers need to heed the counsel of Paul as never before:

> But you, brothers, are not in darkness
> so that this day should surprise you
> like a thief. . . .
> So then, let us not be like others,
> who are asleep,
> but let us be alert and self-controlled. . . .
> putting on faith and love as a breastplate,
> and the hope of salvation as a helmet. . . .
> Therefore encourage one another
> and build each other up. . . .
> 1 Thess. 5:4, 6, 8, 11

---

1. I have been following the year 2000 computer problem and its possible consequences for some time and have been exposed to a wide variety of sources. The most helpful single source of hard information on the vast extent of this potential disaster has been the Internet book by Edwin Yardeni, *Year 2000 Recession?* posted at yardeni.com/y2kbook, version 7.2, July 2, 1998. While Yardeni is probably overly pessimistic, the

hard data that he supplies in support of his arguments must be taken seriously since it comes right from the centers of power: congressional testimony, executive orders and advisements, and high-level business conferences. Relative readiness of corporations and governmental agencies in 1998 and early 1999 is projected into the year 2000 in the "predictive" aspects of this opening scenario.

2. Based on an anonymous article ("Y2K: The Day After") posted by the Fairfax Company of Australia on November 3, 1998, at fairfax.com.au.

3. The summary of the year 2000 problem is based primarily on my own electric utility's newsletter ("18 Months and Counting: UtiliCorp Plans Smooth Transitions into the Year 2000," *Connected*, June 1998, p. 1).

4. For a more detailed summary of the history of this problem see Chris Taylor, "The History and the Hype," *Time*, January 18, 1999, pp. 72-73.

5. Kevin Poulsen, "The Y2K Solution: Run for Your Life!!" *Wired*, August 1998, p. 122.

6. Ibid., p. 165; Ed Yourdon, "Time Bomb 2000," *Y2K News Magazine*, August 1998, p. 12.

7. The problem of embedded chips was noted in Sheryl Brownhill (VP for Information Systems, Robert Thomas Securities, Inc.), "Year 2000 Could Cause Problems Where Least Expected," *Investment Briefings* 12, (Fall 1998): 1; and Jim Seymour (a leading computer analyst) in "My Biggest Worry," *PC Magazine*, October 6, 1998, p. 160.

If you don't enjoy being overly frightened, don't read the following list of critical functions that depend on embedded chips: telephone systems, mobile phones, fax machines, copiers, still and video cameras, heating and ventilating systems, elevators, escalators, safes and vaults, water supply systems, sewage systems, power plants, power grid systems, pacemakers, heart monitors, patient information systems, patient monitoring systems, X-ray equipment, planes, trains, automobiles, buses, trucks, boats, air traffic control instruments, traffic lights, parking meters and ATMs. And I have only mentioned some of the more interesting ones. See Yardeni, part 2, pp. 44-45 for the gory details.

Many people have been unconcerned about this problem because they thought it only affected computers. But the problem of embedded chips draws the Y2K bug out of cyberspace and into the real world of homes and schools and churches.

8. A whole department at Andrews University was informed in 1998 that, since their computers were too old to upgrade and they couldn't afford new ones at this time, they would be cut off from access to the Internet during December of 1999, to make sure that their lack of compliance would not bring down the whole university network at the turn of the millennium.

9. Poulsen, p. 122.

10. Based on Simson L. Garfinkel, "Hooked by the Y2K Bug," *Boston Globe*, October 8, 1998, p. C4.

11. Point raised already by Senator Bob Bennett of Utah, Chairman of the Senate Special Committee on the Year 2000 Technology Problem, on July 6, 1998. Quoted in *Y2K News Magazine*, August 1998, p. 32.

12. Note the urgency with which many U.S. companies have pursued the high-tech

brain-drain: William J. Holstein, "Give Us Your Wired, Your Highly Skilled," *U.S. News and World Report*, October 5, 1998, p. 53.

13. One East African country, as an example, formed a committee in 1998 to investigate problems the country may have in relation to the millennium bug. Their final report on the *problem* is due in April, 2000! Reuters report, "_____ Millennium Bug Report to Finish in April 2000," posted at www.zdnet.com/zdy2k/1998/11/5045.html. (country name in title omitted).

14. Poulsen, p. 124.

15. Ibid. pp. 122-125, 164-167. See also Associated Press report, "Survivalists Await Y2K," posted at news-observer.com, November 3, 1998.

16. Stephanie Armour, "Y2K Means No Vacation," *USA Today*, January 14, 1999, p. 3B.

17. Edwin Yardeni, *Year 2000 Recession?*, version 9.1, November 2, 1998, part 2, p. 49, posted at yardeni.com/y2kbook.

18. Armour, p. 3B.

19. Edward Yardeni, *Year 2000 Recession?*, version 10.0, February 15, 1999, 1, p. 8, posted at yardeni.com/y2kbook.

20. Actually, Senator Bob Bennett of Utah, Chairman of the Senate Special Committee on the Year 2000 Technology Problem, stated on June 12, 1998, that 80% of the electric, oil, and gas utilities in the United States "cannot hope to become Y2K compliant by January 1, 2000." Quoted in *Y2K News Magazine*, August 1998), p. 31. In 1998 Jim Seymour, a leading thinker in the computer field, wrote that the electric-power industry was his greatest concern going into the year 2000 for two reasons; 1) Electricity is vitally important to every other aspect of life today, and 2) The industry was way behind most others at that time in reaching Y2K compliance. Jim Seymour, "My Biggest Worry," *PC Magazine*, October 6, 1998, p. 160.

21. I base this on the actual wording of a 1997 Nuclear Regulatory Commission memo. Quoted in Yardeni, version 7.2, part 1, p. 31.

22. Tony Keyes, "The Impact of Y2K on the Global Economy," *Y2K News Magazine*, August 1998, p. 17.

23. This point was also raised by Senator Bennett on July 12, 1998. See *Y2K News Magazine*, p. 32. See also Seymour, p. 160. Major oil exporters (OPEC) are behind the rest of the world in Y2K preparation. Keyes, p. 17. Fortunately, only 2.2 percent of the powerplants in the U.S. are oil fired; 56.5 percent are coal fired and potential problems with embedded chips in rail switching systems could lead to major problems a month or two after January 1, 2000, (percentages provided by Edison Electric Institute, quoted in *Connected*, the customer newsletter of UtiliCorp United, November, 1998, p. 1.

24. Charles Platt, "America Offline: Inside the Great Blackout of '00'," *Wired*, August 1998, p. 165. An additional problem is that the power grid relies on a sophisticated switching and feedback system which is heavily dependent on embedded chips, many of which can be easily overlooked in any remediation effort. If the chips stop working, the whole system affected by that switch or feedback mechanism could go down, even if power were being produced in sufficient quantities. See Poulsen, p. 164.

25. This scenario was based on Platt, p. 165.

26. There are more than a thousand small telephone companies and hundreds of cellular phone providers. The chances of all being compliant and working well together at the turn of the millennium would seem small, according to Senator Bennett. See *Y2K News Magazine*, p. 33. Bennett was concerned at that time with the lack of any single oversight commission "charged with the task of assuring the reliability and interoperability of the entire network." Ibid., p. 45.

27. Based on Congressional testimony by Senator Bennett on July 31, 1998. See *Y2K News Magazine*, August 1998, p. 33.

28. Keyes, p. 17.

29. "Just in time" manufacturing requires a complex precision that is impossible to manage without computers. The sheer volume of transactions makes it nearly impossible to conduct business on a large scale manually anymore. Tony Keyes, "The Impact of Y2K on the Global Economy," *Y2K News Magazine*, August 1998, p. 17.

30. I am relying here on my cousin, Chuck Paulien, who works for EDT, a computer consulting firm in Colorado, for the insight that the multiple pathways of the Internet will protect it from a Y2K meltdown. Yourdon, on the other hand (p. 12), is convinced that the entire world wide net will be shut down completely for weeks or months by noncompliant components. On a related issue, however, my cousin Chuck is not nearly so optimistic. His company provides hardware and services to the electric industry, and he shares my concern about the power grid.

31. Note the pro and con discussion in Jerry Dunn, "Are You Planning a Flight for Y2K?" *National Geographic Traveler*, September/October1999, p. 22.

32. While major airlines will probably be ready, airports and traffic control systems in some countries seem very unlikely to be ready. Note statements of concern by Dutch airline KLM reported by Steve Alexander, "Airlines, Hospitals Expect to Be Ready for Y2K," posted at startribune.com October 25, 1998.

33. Yardeni, *Year 2000 Recession?*, version 10.0, February1999, part 1, p. 59.

34. Already in the fall of 1998 I received the following advice from a brochure sent by my local bank: "While we believe we will be Y2K compliant, you may want to keep a copy of your December 1999 bank, credit card, or investment account statement, or the last statement prior to 1/1/00, along with copies of any transactions since that statement. All of those records are maintained by computers and Y2K glitches could arise." Sheryl Brownhill (VP for Information Systems, Robert Thomas Securities, Inc.), "Year 2000 Could Cause Problems Where Least Expected," *Investment Briefings*, 12 (Fall 1998): 5.

35. That amount of additional reserves had already been set aside by the Federal Reserve before the end of 1998, according to a *Techweek* report ("Fed Stashes Cash to Prepare for Y2K") posted at techweek.com, November 2, 1998. The Fed also plans to print an extra fifty to seventy-five billion dollars in bank notes during 1999. See John Cloud et al, "The End of the World as We Know It?" *Time*, January 18, 1999, p. 70.

36. Based on Congressional testimony by Senator Bennett on July 6, 1988. See *Y2K News Magazine*, August 1998, p. 32.

37. Alan Greenspan, Chairman of the Federal Reserve Bank testified before the American Congress on Feb. 24, 1998, that even a very small number of non-compliers can cause "a very large problem." (quoted in Yardeni, part 2, p. 3). What could happen to noncompliant banks when the year 2000 arrives? New files may not be recognized as the most recent data, causing current files to be erased or archived as old data. Some customer's billings could be changed from charges to refunds and vice versa. Debt collection and the calculation of interest rates are also likely to be affected. As I write, it is reported that 12 percent of American banks are behind schedule in their Y2K compliance efforts. Most vulnerable seem to be community banks and credit unions. See *Techweek* report ("Fed Stashes Cash to Prepare for Y2K").

38. Armour, p. 3B.

39. On the encouraging side, mortgage systems have been able to recognize the next century for almost 30 years and many credit cards are working fine with expiration dates beyond 2000. See Melissa Wahl, "Banks Try to Exterminate Fears that Y2K Bug Threatens Deposits," *Chicago Tribune*, February 21, 1999, posted at chicagotribune.com, February 22, 1999.

40. "Single Currency Conversion Dwarfs Cost of Date Change," *Computer Weekly News*, posted October 8, 1998, at computerweekly.co.uk.

41. Reuters report, "Social Security Y2K Problems Solved," posted at zdnet.com, December 28, 1998. See also Erich Luening, "Social Security not Bug-free Yet," posted at news.com, December 29, 1998; Jube Shiver Jr., "Clinton, Experts Disagree on Progress of Y2K Glitch Repair," posted at detnews.com, December 29, 1998; and Associated Press report, "Y2K Victory Doesn't Ease Concerns," posted at usatoday.com, December 29, 1998.

42. See Adam Tanner, "Russia, United States Ponder Nuclear Danger of Y2k (sic)," posted at dailynews.yahoo.com, February 21, 1999; idem, "U.S., Russian Experts to Tackle Millennium Bug," Reuters report, posted at infoseek.go.com, February 21, 1999.

43. *The Detroit News*, Technology Section, November 15, 1998, posted at detnews.com.

44. Note the interesting scenarios in Colin D. Standish, "Are *You* Ready for the Y2K Computer Bug?" *Our Firm Foundation*, August 1998, p. 5. The reality in today's world is that information technology is the one thing that differentiates the U.S. from other countries militarily. A year 2000 breakdown would leave the U.S. and its allies in a situation where battlefield superiority is no longer a given. The same would be true of the situation of Israel in the Middle East. Richard Burnett, "Defense Funds Likely to Chase Bug," *Orlando Sentinel*, October 31, 1998, posted as "Efforts to Solve Y2K Flaw Take on Almost Emergency Proportions for Pentagon" at startext.net, November 2, 1998.

45. The U.S. Congress has sought to mitigate this trend to some degree by legislation that encourages prior disclosure. See Margaret Kane, "Senate Passes Bill to Protect Companies from Y2K Liabilities," posted at zdnet.com, September 29, 1998. See also "Y2K: The Day After," posted at fairfax.com.au, November 3, 1998, which anticipates similar problems in Australia. Actually the problem is being foreshadowed by an acceleration of software lawsuits already in 1998 and 1999, as companies seek to pin Y2K costs on suppliers, who then

try to get reimbursement from their insurance companies! See Peter Coffee, "Y2K Marathon Starts Its Last Mile," posted at zdnet.com, December 21, 1998. Insurance companies in turn seek to defend themselves from Y2K litigation by excluding year 2000 problems from eligibility for insurance reimbursement. See Jenny Sinclair, "Millennium Bug Woes Expected to Linger," posted at fairfax.com.au, November 3, 1998. After the year 2000 begins, the legal focus should turn to problems in products whose function or availability is dependent on computers in some way. See also Lisa M. Bowman, "IBM Hit by Y2K Suit," posted at zdnet.com, December 22, 1998.

46. "Y2K: The Day After," posted at fairfax.com.au, November 3, 1998.

47. Yardeni, *Year 2000 Recession?*, version 10.0, February 15, 1999, part 1, pp. 4, 21-22.

48. Ibid., p. 5.

49. This plan was already in place by 1998; Keyes, p. 17.

50. Clint Willis, "Y2K: Countdown to Crisis," *Mutual Funds Magazine*, October 1998, p. 54.

51. Paul Bedard, Washington Whispers, *U.S. News and World Report*, November 9, 1998, p. 11.

52. For an overview of the scenario of final events as outlined in the Book of Revelation, see my book *What the Bible Says About the End-Time* (Hagerstown, Md.: Review and Herald, 1994), especially pp. 105-150.

53. Fiscal year budgeters, who depend on date-sensitive computers and programs, will get an inkling of their Y2K readiness on July 1 or October 1, 1999. Furthermore, since many early programmers used the code "99" to tell computers to shut down, problems may occur on September 9, 1999 (9/9/99) or on April 9, 1999 (99th day of 1999). See Michael J. Miller (editor of *PC Magazine*), "Five Y2K Myths," posted at zdnet.com, September 14, 1998. See also Terry Brock, "Six Steps for Surviving the Coming Y2K Storm," posted at amcity.com, November 2, 1998.

54. Cloud et al, p. 70. The stock market tends to discount potential bad news in advance and often to the extreme. If the Y2K problem turns out to be less severe than the market believed it would be, the month of January, 2000 could actually be a positive one in the financial markets. And retailing may experience its own brief bonanza in the latter half of 1999 as citizens take precaution by stocking up on supplies of dried foods, batteries, and other essentials.

55. Late-1998 estimates of total cost, just for the U.S. and ten European countries ranged as high as 858 billion dollars. Bruce Caldwell, "Y2K Estimates Rise," *InformationWeek*, November 16, 1998, posted at techweb.com.

56. Yardeni, *Year 2000 Recession?*, version 10.0, part 1, pp. 4, 50-51; Cloud et al, "The End of the World as We Know It?" *Time*, January 18, 1990, pp. 63-64. Reassurances from government are not entirely comforting considering the governmental tendency to downplay disasters in order to avoid popular panic.

57. Kevin Lemke, the founder of Computerland in Grand Forks, ND, anticipates two or three days of failures in phone and electricity service, followed by a few weeks of intermittent problems. Ron Braley, a computer systems administrator, is more concerned about the banking, finance, and world trade. See Steve Foss, "Y2K: Are We Safe?" *Grand Forks Herald*,

February 21, 1999, posted at gfherald.com. Dick Mills, an electrical engineer who advises the power industry, says that the electric grid will provide "power to most of the people most of the time in 2000," but that people should be prepared for blackouts of up to 72 hours. See Dick Mills, "Dick Mills' Y2K Power Prognosis" and "Balkanization of the Grid," posted at y2ktimebomb.com, January 22, 1999.

58. Note the following from an investment newsletter sent out by my local bank: "Whether it is called the 'bug,' 'millennium bug' or just 'Y2K,' the problem does exist. It is real, it is widespread and it could affect all of us." Sheryl Brownhill (VP for Information Systems, Robert Thomas Securities, Inc.), "Year 2000 Could Cause Problems Where Least Expected," *Investment Briefings* 12 (Fall 1998): 1. A lone dissenting voice was raised by James Coates of the *Chicago Tribune*, who offered in the November 8, 1998 issue of the newspaper his concern that the "voice of reason (has been) drowned out in a sea of Y2K scaremongers" (posted on startext.net, November 12, 1998). I hope he is right, but he offered no evidence for optimism except to note that the majority of those warning about the computer date change are Y2K consultants, which means they have some financial interest in people taking the problem seriously.

CHAPTER 2

A Decade of Titanic Excitement

Just about everyone seems to be catching the Millennium Bug. The approaching year 2000 is attracting increasing attention in both the secular media and in the Adventist community. The almost magical power of a round number has combined with a series of extraordinary events like El Niño, the Asian crisis, and Y2K to create a sense of profound anticipation. In times like these, biblical predictions of the end of the world sometimes take center stage in surprising places.

HOW WE GOT HERE

The years leading up to the end of the millennium have witnessed some amazing events. For me the first anticipation of something special was the afternoon of October 19, 1987, sometimes known as Black Friday, as I sat by the radio hearing reports of panic on the New York Stock Exchange. A drop of more than 500 points (about 22 percent of total value) on the Dow occurred in a matter of hours. Recollections of 1929 and the Great Depression passed through many minds that weekend, and an even greater downdraft the next week was barely averted. Few people realize how close the American economy came to disaster that week.

The perspective of hindsight helps us to see that this event was merely a momentary loss of confidence in what has otherwise been a seventeen-year (and counting as I write) bull market. But at the time I pondered deeply about what might have been. The fact that the near collapse of the market coincided with a prediction, circulated among many Adventists, that the great End-Time Jubilee would occur in October, 1987, was not lost on some minds.[1] Nevertheless, this first anticipation of extraordinary events proved to be a false alarm.

Far more significant were the events of 1989. I never dreamed in 1980 that the Berlin Wall would come down in my lifetime, much less in my father's lifetime.[2] How many times I had looked with longing at the Brandenburg Gate standing in the midst of no-man's land, never dreaming that I would be able to walk through it freely in the 90s! The sudden fall of communism throughout Eastern Europe took most people totally by surprise. Since that year we can look back on a living, current model for the statement, "Great changes are soon to take place in our world, and the final movements will be rapid ones" (Ellen G. White, *Testimonies for the Church*, vol. 9, p. 11).

Not long after the changes in Eastern Europe came the Gulf War. In the midst of a brief episode of destroying and killing came a stunning confirmation of the changes brought into our world by technology. Tank battles on a large scale lasted for months in World War II.[3] In the Gulf War, such battles were decided in a matter of hours, sometimes in minutes. In techno-war the side with the superior technology has the capability to wipe out the other side so rapidly that no serious counter-response is possible. While all this was going on, people in Israel and Saudi Arabia literally held their breath wondering if the next SCUD missile would deliver a weapon of mass destruction.

In the wake of the Gulf War, President Bush declared the existence of an American-led "new world order." It was expected that the major powers of the world would now work together politically, and that warfare would be reduced to economic rivalry and an occasional terrorist attack. To many Adventist minds this sounded like the great end-time coalition of Revelation.

The "New World Order" already seems, however, a thing of the past. Events in places like Somalia, Rwanda, and Bosnia look much more like a New World Disorder. We see intensifying resistance to American global power by a number of "secondary" powers, such as China, Russia, India, Pakistan, France, and Saudi Arabia, not to mention Iran and Iraq, of course.[4] Many of these powers seek to establish local spheres of influence to counter-balance the erratic use of American world power.[5] And America's use of power is increasingly erratic because its political and economic interests have less and less in common with each other in a networked world. The result of this New World Disorder is a return to the old days before the Cold War. The development of new regional alliances has the potential for devastating regional conflicts, just like in the old days before the Cold War.[6] So Bush's declaration of a New World Order was certainly premature.[7]

Shortly after the Gulf War people began to become aware of a development that may be far more earthshaking than anything that happened in 1989, the Internet. For years we had been aware of an incredible explosion of knowledge and publication. It has become incredibly hard for anyone to keep up with the knowledge explosion, even in the narrowest of fields. Suddenly the whole world is wired and it no longer takes a Ph.D. to find out almost anything you want to know from a desktop in Timbuktu or anywhere else.[8]

The Internet has greater implications for the human race than most people realize. It has totally changed the way we do business. Imagine banks today trying to keep track of accounts with typewriters and handwritten notes! Imagine airlines keeping track of today's level of flights and seats by phone, pencil and paper, and traditional radar! The Internet is even changing the way we do education. Sooner than we think, traditional campuses may be a thing of the past and "home schooling" of some sort a way of life right up to the Ph.D. level.[9] The Internet is even changing the way people learn and process their knowledge. No one knows exactly where it all will lead, but barring a fatal shutdown on January 1, 2000, or some other worldwide catastrophe, the Internet may yet prove to be the most significant development of the millennium, not just the decade.

In the midst of all these exciting developments has come the most ambitious and most popular pope in recent memory. His every movement and his every speech are instant news. He is not only the dominant religious figure in today's world, he is highly influential in the political realm as well. The events of 1989 were clearly far larger than any one person could have engineered. There is no question that Pope John Paul II influenced events and must be taken seriously on the world stage.[10] For Adventists, this is no minor development.

Then in 1998, this same pope weighed in on the Sabbath-Sunday question in light of "the threshold of the Great Jubilee of the Year 2000."[11] In his pastoral letter *Dies Domini* he laments the crisis of Sunday observance including low attendance at the Sunday liturgy. He believes that the decline of Sunday observance threatens the very viability of the Catholic Church in the coming millennium. Of particular interest to Adventists, he argues both for the moral obligation of Sunday observance and the need to encourage legislation which will facilitate compliance with that obligation. He makes the secular argument that Sunday laws are especially needed today because of the psychological, social, and ecological stresses humanity faces as a result of technological development. But he also calls upon the precedent of Constantine's first Sunday law back in the fourth century, a precedent that Adventists can only view with alarm. These developments certainly sound a lot like what the book *Great Controversy* (pages 573-581) predicted over a hundred years ago.

These exciting events combined in the 1990s with a number of remarkable natural events to create "titanic" excitement in some quarters. Weather studies have indicated that the three warmest years of the entire millennium all occurred in the 1990s. This is certainly an ominous portent in the light of the "global warming" alarms many scientists have been setting off. The El Niño phenomenon became widely understood for the first time, in part because the El Niños of the last decade of the millennium had such a strong and widespread impact. While Michigan basked in unaccustomed sunshine the entire winter of 1997-1998, for example, the sunshine state of California was overwhelmed with gray clouds and rain.[12] If you lived in either of those states at the time you had to wonder.

Other natural events were also greeted with some trepidation. By some accounts at least, the ozone hole over the southern hemisphere was increasing.[13] Some reports indicate a similar decline in atmospheric ozone beginning to occur in the Northern Hemisphere. Who would have thought that just being outside could be dangerous? If that isn't bad enough, a comet recently struck the planet Jupiter, one of our near neighbors, and an asteroid recently passed within a few hundred thousand miles of earth. Even an average sized asteroid could easily destroy life on the earth as we know it. While Adventists do not believe that world history will end on account of an asteroid impact, Adventist writers have raised the possibility that such an impact could be a major factor in precipitating the final events of earth's history.[14]

For Adventists themselves, a further development causes one to wonder if "these times" are not of greater import than ever before. Never before in our history has there been so much confusion and diversity in the church. Group after group rises up to press its distinctive agenda on the church. They assert, respectively, that the church will fail unless it centers its message on the 1888 presentations of Waggoner and Jones, or proclaims the sole validity of the King James Bible, or accepts the sinful human nature of Christ, or promotes final-generation perfection, or mandates the exclusive expression "Yahweh" for God, or promotes a particular view of women's ordination. Adventist scholars have split into separate professional societies with different perceptions of what the church needs today.[15] Church leaders are sometimes painfully divided between those who feel that church planting is the wave of the future and those who prefer to grow existing churches.

Up until 1980, criticism of the church, its leaders, and its mission was largely confined to the so-called "liberal" elements in the church. But since that time many conservatives have been outdoing the liberals in their disrespect for church structure and authority and the ministers, teachers and administrators who strive to keep that structure together. One conference president told me of letters he had received from some of the more conservative members in his conference. They combined Spirit of Prophecy quotations with personal attacks that included four-letter expletives! And all sides seem to be increasingly calling into question the church's structure and its use of finances. In times like these the toughest job in the church is in administration. Leading Adventists these days is like holding a tiger by the tail!

Given the new realities in the world and in the church, and given the awesome approach of the year 2000, it is not surprising that many Adventists are wondering if we are beginning to witness the final events of this world's history. And they are not alone in this conviction. . . .

THE CURRENT SITUATION

Twenty years ago, as a pastor in New York City, I had quite a bit of success reaching the secular community with outreach programs related to health and longevity. For example, one mailing of fewer than ten thousand flyers brought in a crowd of 75 people, few of whom had had any prior contact with the Adventist Church. When the conference launched a citywide satellite evangelism campaign with George Vandeman, I decided to work that into a series of Revelation Seminars. A couple of major donations allowed us to send out 62,000 flyers this time. A total of seven people showed up (at one of the three sites, where more than 15,000 flyers had been distributed, not a single person showed up for the meetings)! It became obvious to all concerned that the book of Revelation and end-time events were not major matters of discussion in the secular community of New York City at that time.

All that has changed. The events of the last decade or so, the widespread availability of videos and mass-market paperbacks, and the approach of the magical number 2000, have all put the book of Revelation and the end of the world high on people's agendas, even in non-Christian circles.[16] This juncture of popular interest in both the book of Revelation and the end of the world is confirmed by two wildly popular movies of the 1990s, *Terminator 2* and *Armageddon.*

Terminator 2: Judgment Day (the full title as introduced to theaters in 1992) completed a pair of violent action thrillers that proved to be prophetic of the current situation. Together the *Terminator* movies replay the basic scenario of the book of Revelation in a contemporary setting of runaway computers precipitating nuclear war. The salvation of the world depends on a woman with an unborn child, heroic self-sacrifice, and the timely appearance of a lake of fire at the end.[17] This contemporary version of the plot of Revelation struck tremendous emotional chords in today's world.[18]

Then in the summer of 1998 came *Armageddon*. While scientifically inaccurate, the movie portrayed the potential end of history occurring through the impact of a huge asteroid with the surface of the earth. It was not even necessary to unpack for the audience the meaning of the title *Armageddon* which was, of course, drawn from the Apocalypse. The book of Revelation is today widely associated with the end of the world, and the end of the world is increasingly thought of as a real and even imminent possibility.

The book of Revelation, therefore, is far more influential in current popular culture than most people realize. The very term "Apocalypse," for example, has become a synonym for "Doomsday;" a reference to the end of the world, whether by violence, economic catastrophe, or natural disaster. The term apocalypse has been used with regard to global warming,[19] the health effects of proximity to electric power lines,[20] urban population growth,[21] increased traffic on the Internet,[22] welfare reform,[23] and even alpine snowboards![24] The term is also used as a title for recent novels,[25] for a musical recording by, of all things, a Moroccan folk band,[26] and with reference to court congestion and delays,[27] the demise of the sun,[28] overpopulation in general,[29] AIDS,[30] and the unfortunate events in Waco, Texas, back in 1993.[31]

The book of Revelation also turns up in the world of music. The rock star formerly known as Prince, for example, often laces his music with verbal images from the book of Revelation. The lyrics from the hit song "7" include references to an angel who comes down from heaven, a decree declaring those who champion love are blasphemers, a river of blood, and a new city with streets of gold where there is no death.

Further popular images which have their source in the book of Revelation include the concept of Antichrist (a terrifying end-time tyrant based on the descriptions of the beast of chapter 13), the falling star Wormwood (a demonic figure in *The Screwtape Letters*, by C. S. Lewis), the four apocalyptic horsemen (applied tongue-in-cheek to a highly-successful backfield on the Notre Dame football team), the end-time millennium (a Latin term for the thousand year period that comes at the close of earth's history in the Apocalypse), and the horrifying nothingness of the Abyss (a bottomless pit which is both the source and the destiny of all evil in the world). Even more images that have influenced contemporary society include the idea of a mystic Babylon, a New Jerusalem, the Alpha and the Omega, the Mark of the Beast, and the cryptic number of the Antichrist, 666.

Due to the tremendous influence of the Apocalypse in today's world, there has also been a resurgence of scholarly interest in the book at major centers of learning such as Harvard, Notre Dame, and the University of Chicago, and in scholarly societies such as the Society of Biblical Literature and the Chicago Society for Biblical Research.

Along with interest in the book of Revelation there is a parallel interest in the end of the world and how that might come about. Like John, the author of Revelation, people today think of themselves as living, at least potentially, in the last generation of earth's history. Over two decades ago the Club of Rome (a group of scientists) predicted that within thirty years civilization would collapse under the weight of increasing population and the lack of food. Since that time a multitude of survival-threatening problems have come to our attention. In 1973-1974 and 1979 major energy shortages raised world consciousness to the fact that natural resources are limited. The "Greenhouse Effect" (a gradual warming of the earth due to the effects of pollution) threatens to melt the polar ice caps and inundate coastal areas. The destruction of the world's last sizable rain forest in Brazil raises questions about the earth's ability to maintain the necessary supply of oxygen in its atmosphere to sustain animal and human life. The movie *Independence Day* raised the specter of hostile alien invasion. The movies *Deep Impact* and *Armageddon* alerted the general populace to the possibility that alien objects, such as comets, giant meteorites, and asteroids should be a concern.[32] The threat of germ and chemical warfare, toxic waste dumps, the destruction of the earth's ozone layer, terrorism, and such new diseases as AIDS and Ebola have made everyone well aware of human mortality.

But the apocalyptic threat that still poses the most terror for modern civilization is the awesome horror of nuclear war. Nuclear apocalypse has become a recurring theme in both the sciences and the arts. The *Bulletin of the Atomic Scientists* has maintained a constant warning of the end with its famous "minutes to midnight" clock, recently scaled back because of developments in the former Soviet Union. But while optimism may now reign in some quarters, the nuclear arsenals in the former Soviet Union remain largely intact, while the systems controlling them have become increasingly unstable. The chances of former Soviet weapons getting into terrorist hands, or of some "uncontrollable" nation developing its own arsenal seem less a matter of "if" than of "when." Lesser powers like India and Pakistan seek "great power" status through the development of nuclear weapons, which could easily end up being used to settle regional disputes. There is even the Terminator-like specter of a programming malfunction on the part of one or more computers that run the world's nuclear arsenals.

That the survival of humanity is now in question is amply illustrated also in the arts. Robert Morris, a New York City artist, has become famous for sculptures that illustrate piles of human body parts, as if torn apart by a nuclear holocaust. Alexander Melamid and Vitaly Komar stunned the art world with their painting *Scenes from the Future—the Guggenheim*. This painting depicts the broken-down remains of the Guggenheim Museum in New York surrounded by a nuclear desert.[33] Movies such as *The Day After* and *The Road Warrior* not only depict the horror of nuclear destruction, but explore the nature of life afterward, if such can be imagined. Thus a recent philosophical trend is "post-apocalypticism," which considers nuclear destruction inevitable and seeks to understand what kind of future humanity has in the light of that impending reality.

As the Apocalypse makes clear, this generation is not the first to perceive that it could be the last. The difference is that this is the first generation that has perceived that the end could come without a God.[34] Somehow the idea that God could bring about the end allows for the possibility that He could save as well. But the secular apocalypse faced by this generation could be the result of an accident of history, even the random madness of a terrorist with a "Doomsday Machine." Thus we face the end as potentially an "abyss of meaninglessness." Perhaps the human condition was best expressed in the words of the Terminator itself, a computer-generated being, part human and part machine, "It's in your nature to destroy yourselves."

If you're not feeling just a little breathless right now, you have a stronger constitution than I could dream of! Not only is the world of today far different than it was twenty years ago, there is every reason to think that we have little idea of what it would be like in twenty years more, if time should last. The changes are vast, irreversible and totally beyond human control.

RESPONSE TO TITANIC EXCITEMENT

If the times in which we live are exciting even from a secular perspective, is it any wonder that Bible-believing Adventists are particularly attentive to these events? Is it any wonder that Bible-believing Adventists might consider the possibility that these events signal Jesus' intention to return in the immediate future? Is it time to discover the date of Jesus' return? Is it possible to know that this is truly the final generation of earth's history? Many Adventists think so and believe that they can prove it.

Perhaps you have heard that the fortieth Jubilee[35] since the time of Christ occurred during the 1990s. Just as slaves were freed and the land restored in the ancient type, so it seems reasonable to suggest that Jesus might choose to return during a modern-day year of Jubilee. While the several dates that many have suggested for this fortieth Jubilee have already passed, it is certainly possible to consider that the exciting times ushered in by the 90s may have something to do with a heavenly Jubilee timetable.

Perhaps you have heard that the seven heads of the beast in Revelation 17 represent seven popes beginning with the year 1929. Depending on how people treat the brief reign of John Paul I in 1978, it is thought that Pope John Paul II is either the last pope of earth's history or the next to last.

Perhaps you have heard about the hitchhiker picked up by a couple of Adventist boys. They invited him into the back seat and took off down the highway. The stranger proceeded to say (without them having revealed anything about themselves), "You Adventists are really deceived,

Jesus is coming sooner than you think." When they whipped their heads around in surprise, the stranger had disappeared! Stories like this suggest to some, at least, the possibility that angels might be preparing us for the imminent End of all things.

Perhaps you have heard about the rapid increase in apparitions of "Mary" over the last couple of decades. In an increasing number of these "appearances" prophecies about the End have been delivered, declaring that the End is at hand and that momentous events will take place leading up to and during the year 2000.[36] With my own eyes I recently saw a billboard at the shrine memorializing the home of Mary near ancient Ephesus in Turkey. The sign said, "Come Back on August 15, 2000 A.D. and Meet Jesus!"

Speaking of the year 2000 once again, perhaps you've heard that the earth is about 6000 years old as the year 2000 approaches. Some have suggested (my mother, for one, brought this up when I was just a little boy) that biblical typology points to 6000 years of sinful history followed by a thousand-year "sabbath" of resolution to the sin problem. So a number of Adventists think that the year 2000 may somehow be connected with final events.[37]

Adventists are not alone in their focus on the year 2000. Damien Thompson has demonstrated how latent year 2000 excitement has played a role in the charismatic outburst known as the "Toronto Blessing."[38] In Roman Catholic circles, Pope John Paul II has ordered a vast program of preparation for the "Great Jubilee" of the year 2000.[39] The date is increasingly mentioned as well in relation to the Marian apparitions.[40] For New Agers the year 2000 comes smack in the middle of the twenty-five year transition from the Age of Pisces to the Age of Aquarius.[41]

SEEKING AN ADVENTIST RESPONSE

In light of the incredible events happening now and soon to happen, how should we respond to creative attempts to determine more or less when Jesus is going to come? Can that type of attention to current events be a blessing that calls us to great fervor and preparation? Or is there a dark side that we need to avoid? In the face of "titanic excitement" both inside and outside of the church, a sober reflection on history, experience, and God's revelations about the End are a must.

I have tried to portray the current excitement in both the church and the wider world as accurately as possible. I strongly feel the pull of that excitement and am tempted to yield to it and proclaim with certainty that our times are the very last ones, and that our generation will truly be the last generation of this earth's history. But before we succumb to the temptation to go down that road, let me share another side to reality in the chapters which follow.

---

1. Chet Wolfe, *Then Commenced the Jubilee When the Land Should Rest.* This undated 36-page newsprint flyer arrived in my office sometime during the mid-1980s. Wolfe projected the beginning of the millennium (the last jubilee and presumably the second coming of Christ) to October 3, 1987.

2. Both of my parents trace their heritage to Germany, and I still have many relatives there, although I myself was born in New York City. I had the opportunity to live in Germany in 1968-69 and paid many visits to the Berlin Wall.

3. I am thinking particularly of the Battle of Kursk in 1943.

4. Summarized in a "Global Intelligence Update," posted at stratfor.com, July 6, 1998. According to Stratfor's 1999 Annual Forecast (posted January 3, 1999), a major global counterweight to the United States is likely to form with France, Russia, and China being the major players and Japan, India (on the problem of India see intelligence update posted on January 15, 1999), and Germany (on Germany and Japan see intelligence update posted on February 22, 1999) caught somewhere in the middle.

5. A couple of interesting recent regional alliances are India's overtures to Israel in order to counterbalance the Islamic threat of Pakistani nukes, Iran's successful wooing of Saudi Arabia as a counterbalance to American and Iraqi interests in the region ("Global Intelligence Update," posted July 31, 1998 at stratfor.com), and the Russian-Japanese "coalition of economic cripples" seeking to counterbalance the overwhelming economic power of the United States and Western Europe in the current economy ("Global Intelligence Update," posted July 13, 1998 at stratfor.com).

6. In the Middle East Cyprus is becoming a flashpoint with the potential to spark a major regional war that could involve (in order of likelihood) Greece, Syria, Russia, and Iran on one side, and Turkey, Israel, Jordan, and conceivably even (gasp) Iraq on the other ("Global Intelligence Update," posted Sept. 10, 1998 at stratfor.com). A further update on November 25, 1998 noted Greek overtures toward the possibility of Egypt joining in. The potential spread of Taleban-style fundamentalism from Afghanistan has united China, Russia, Iran, and Uzbekistan against Afghanistan, Kazakstan, and Pakistan, while at the same time Pakistan's interests are united with China's against India ("Global Intelligence Update," posted October 8, 1998 at stratfor.com).

7. A shocking summary of the breakdown of political consensus at the close of the

millennium is outlined in "The End of the New World Order," a "Global Intelligence Update," posted August 31, 1998, posted at stratfor.com.

8. Yes, there is such a place, located in the Sahara nation of Mali. Timbuktu was once the capital of a major empire, but has now become a symbol of isolation and irrelevance.

9. This statement is so radical it scares the daylights of me! But see Peter H. Wagschal, "Distance Education Comes to the Academy: But Are We Asking the Right Questions?" *Distance Education Report*, July 1998, pp. 1-3. It may be years before educators catch up, but the Internet changes everything!

10. Note the fascinating mixture of news reporting and speculation in Malachi Martin, *The Keys of This Blood: The Struggle for World Dominion Between Pope John Paul II, Mikhail Gorbachev, and the Capitalist West* (NY: Simon and Schuster, 1990). While most of Martin's ambitious predictions have proved incorrect, the sense that he is somehow an "insider" into the Pope's plans has made this book a bestseller among Adventists.

11. This brief summary of the pope's pastoral letter is greatly indebted to the Internet postings of Samuele Bacchiocchi in the summer of 1998. These can be obtained from him at samuele@andrews.edu.

12. Normally around Andrews University the thermometer rarely climbs above 32 degrees Fahrenheit (0 degrees Celcius) at any time from December 15 through January 31. In the entire winter of 1997-1998 I remember only *one* day in which the high was below freezing! In the last ten years I have lived here I can't remember a single "golf day" from November 10 through March 31. In the winter of 1997-1998 I played golf four times and could have done so a dozen times more if I had wanted to! Something strange (but delightful to us) in the neighborhood.

13. I have had a chance to spend time in South New Zealand during ozone hole season. Sunburn times are announced in the news, and usually range from 15-25 minutes! Imagine a painful sunburn in only fifteen minutes of exposure! I can testify from personal experience that even a moment's sunshine can be almost painful without the protection that the ozone layer provides over most of the earth.

14. Marvin Moore, *The Coming Great Calamity* (Nampa, Idaho: Pacific Press, 1997), pp. 47-71; Larry Wilson, *Warning! Revelation Is About to Be Fulfilled* (Bellbrook, Ohio: Wake Up America Seminars, 1997), pp. 59-86.

15. It should be noted here that many Adventist scholars prefer to participate in both societies whenever that is possible.

16. Kyle, p. 99.

17. The many ways in which the *Terminator* movies play off the scenario of the book of Revelation are amply documented in Roland Boer, "Christological Slippage and Ideological Structures in Schwartzenegger's *Terminator*," *Semeia* 69/70 (1995):173-174.

18. Michael Hirschorn declared the original *Terminator* movie the most important film of the 1980s in *Esquire*, September 1990), pp. 116-117. The great popularity of *Terminator 2* is evidenced by its $204 million dollars in theater receipts in North America alone.

19. Michael D. Lemonick, "Heading for Apocalypse?" *Time*, October 2, 1995, p. 54;

cf. review of *Earth First!: Environmental Apocalypse,* by S. Hollenhorst in *Choice,* July-August 1996, p. 1816.

20. Jon Palfreman, "Apocalypse Not," *Technology Review* 55 (April 1996): 24.

21. Fred Pearce, "Urban Apocalypse Postponed?" *New Scientist,* June 1, 1996, p. 4.

22. Richard Overton, "Internet Apocalypse," *PC World,* July 1996, p. 45.

23. Jill Nelson, "Apocalypse Now," *The Nation,* August 26, 1996, p. 10.

24. Dana White, "Rip rides," *Skiing,* February 1992, p. 91.

25. *The Apocalypse Watch,* by Robert Ludlum; and *Night of the Apocalypse,* by Daniel Easterman. In the book *Writing the Apocalypse: Historical Vision in Contemporary U.S. and Latin American Fiction* (Cambridge: Cambridge University Press, 1993), Lois Parkinson Zamora surveys more than a dozen recent "apocalyptic" novels. See the review by John Mowat in *Journal of American Studies* 28 (August 1994): 301-302.

26. See the review of "Apocalypse Across the Sky," a CD recording by the Master Musicians of Jajouka in *The New York Times,* July 12, 1992, section 2, p. H23.

27. "Apocalypse When?" *The National Law Journal,* January 9, 1995, p. A20.

28. Malcolm W. Brown, "New Look at Apocalypse," *The New York Times,* September 20, 1994, p. 85.

29. "Apocalypse Soon," *The Economist,* July 23, 1994, p. A25.

30. "African Apocalypse," *Time,* July 6, 1992, p. 21.

31. Richard Woodbury, "After the Apocalypse," *Time,* January 17, 1994, p 17; "Children of the Apocalypse," *Newsweek,* May 3, 1993, p. 30.

32. This possibility was raised years earlier by the cover story in *Newsweek,* November 23, 1992.

33. Davis, pp. 197-199.

34. Bernard Brandon Scott, *Hollywood Dreams and Biblical Stories* (Minneapolis: Fortress Press, 1994), p. 199; Kyle, p. 167.

35. The biblical Jubilee (Leviticus 25) occurred as the climax of seven "weeks" of seven years each. At the beginning of the Jubilee year (the forty-ninth or fiftieth year in the sequence) all slaves were freed and all property reverted to the original owner or their descendants. It seems reasonable to suggest that this day of liberation is a fitting model for what Christ does for His people at the Second Coming.

36. Note the accounts in Moore, *The Coming Great Calamity,* pp. 92-122.

37. Interestingly enough, the new millennium actually begins in A.D. 2001, not in A.D. 2000, Kyle, p. 190.

38. Damien Thompson, *The End of Time: Faith and Fear in the Shadow of the Millennium* (Hanover, N.H.: University Press of New England, 1996), p. 142.

39. Ibid., pp. 167-168.

40. Ibid., pp. 182-183.

41. Running from the harmonic convergence of 1987 to 2012. See Thompson, pp. 191-225 and Kyle, pp. 155-156.

CHAPTER 3

Going Beyond the Evidence

The times in which we live are exciting. The speed with which things change and new developments occur takes your breath away sometimes. You can't blame anyone for wondering whether these extraordinary circumstances might be leading us up to the final events of human history. So it comes as no surprise that some Adventists have been looking for biblical, natural, political, economic, religious, and Spirit of Prophecy reasons to demonstrate that this is in fact the final hour, that Jesus is about to come.

Oh, how much I want Jesus to come! Though this world is still full of beauty and joy, even the best of times doesn't last very long. There is also much suffering, abuse, and heartache in the world—far too much! How I wish the future were now! But I have to constantly remind myself that God's thoughts are not my thoughts, and my thoughts are not God's thoughts (Isa. 55:6-9). My desire to be with the Lord cannot by itself make it happen. The excitement of current events in themselves cannot make it happen. In spite of my desire for Jesus to come soon I see five major problems with current attempts to demonstrate just where we are in the final scheme of things. The Year 2000, Jubilees, angel visitations, the succession of popes, Marian apparitions, etc., are all most interesting to observe. But as impressive as they may be, none of them seems to be the "smoking gun" that reveals with any certainty that the final times are upon us.

LEAPS OF LOGIC

There is a common denominator in all these attempts to somehow calculate the timing of the end. Each of them requires a "leap of logic" to follow the argument to a conclusion. There is usually some kind of basis in the Bible or the Spirit of Prophecy for aspects of the author's argument. At some crucial point, however, you have to accept a basic assumption, or make some kind of intellectual jump, without clear evidence, in order to reach the desired conclusion. That just isn't good enough. Spiritual survival in the End time requires more than leaps of logic. It must be based on a clear "Thus saith the Lord."

The assertion that Jesus will come after six thousand years of earth's history and usher in a millennial Sabbath is a very appealing one from a logical and biblical perspective. It finds a basis in the biblical teaching of a recurring weekly Sabbath, and in the sabbatical year practices of the ancient Hebrew economy (one year in seven the land was to lie fallow). But anticipating the coming of Jesus sometime around the year 2000 on this basis requires at least two major leaps of logic. For one thing, the Bible nowhere connects the coming of Jesus with the six thousandth year of earth's history. Furthermore, nowhere in the Bible is the exact age of the earth stated, nor is it readily calculable from Scripture. So while the 6000-year theory is appealing to the heart, you have to jump beyond the evidence to make your case. We will take a closer look at a popular version of this theory in chapter 5.

A similar situation exists with popular scenarios regarding an End-time Jubilee calendar. The idea that the second coming of Jesus represents a liberation from servitude in a sin-filled world is, once again, theologically attractive. And there are many reasons to applaud the economic and humanitarian benefits of the divine institution of the Jubilee in the ancient Israelite theocracy.[1] But basing a study of the timing of the end on the Jubilee calendar also requires leaps of logic.

For Jubilee calculations to provide a reliable basis for Christian action today you have to have a fixed starting point, such as the date of Creation or the Exodus. But there is no scriptural basis for certainty regarding the date of either the Creation or the Exodus. Even conservative scholars have points of difference on how to read the biblical evidence, and the archaeological evidence for the timing of the Exodus is also inconclusive. And even if the Exodus date could be determined, it is not likely that Jubilee cycles would have begun until all twelve tribes were settled in the land, more than forty years later.

Even if you could start your Jubilee calculation with a fixed date, such as the crucifixion of Jesus (A.D. 31), however, you would still lack a clear scriptural statement indicating that Jubilees forecast the timing of Jesus' return.[2] Attempting to calculate the timing of the End on the basis of Jubilee calendars requires leaps of logic that, in my mind, invalidate its usefulness as a basis for timing the End.

The middle part of Revelation 17 has always intrigued interpreters. I once held a doctoral seminar specifically on that difficult chapter. Five bright researchers wrestled with the chapter in the original language for an accumulated time of nearly a thousand hours. They found the imagery, particularly in verses 7 to 11, so problematic that after their research they felt even less certain about many details than they had before. Revelation 17 is without a doubt one of the more difficult passages of the Bible to understand. Spiritual survival in the End time must be based on the clear texts of the Bible.

Having said that, it is not difficult to rule out the view that the seven kings of Revelation 17 represent popes in the twentieth century. Prophetic visions such as those in Daniel and Revelation can take a prophet here and there in the course of time, but *explanations of those visions always come in terms of the prophet's own time and place.* In Dan. 2, for example, most of the image concerns things far into the future from the perspective of Daniel and Nebuchadnezzar. *But the explanation is rooted in the time when the vision was explained.*[3] The purpose of the explanation is so that the prophet (or in this case prophet and king) can understand. Time references within the explanation, therefore, are from the perspective of the prophet's time and place. So when the angel says to John, "Five have fallen, one is, the other has not yet come" (Rev. 17:10), the point of reference is John's time, not ours. Whoever these seven kings are, five of them were already past from John's point of view, this could not be a series of individuals in the twentieth century.[4] As with the previous two proposals, here again logic must leap beyond the text in order to establish the point.

With angelic hitchhikers we move beyond the realm of biblical interpretation and into the realm of charismatic evidences for the nearness of the End. I have no personal basis for knowing whether these encounters ever actually occurred and if they did, I have no way to know whether the angels were actually from God or not. I do know this. These stories have been around for a long time. I first heard one in the year 1967. At that time most of my friends and I did not expect time to last more than five or ten additional years. Whoever the angel was that said, "Jesus is coming sooner than you think," that angel was wrong. Time has continued for more than thirty years since. To base our expectations of the end on stories that come unsubstantiated over the grapevine (now known as the Internet) and without biblical support is very risky business. To me this, too, requires a leap of logic.

This brings us to the "prophecies" related to apparitions of Mary. I find Adventist fascination with these to be amazing. For starters, Adventists don't for a minute believe that these apparitions are genuine. They believe that Mary is sleeping in her grave and doesn't have a clue about when she will be resurrected or about any other subject for that matter. In order to gain useful information from these apparitions, then, Adventists are forced to the conclusion that these apparitions and the prophecies that accompany them are deceptions of the devil.[5] But I for one would hate to base any aspect of my faith on evidence that originates with a deception of Satan! For all we know it is serving his purposes to get people excited about the year 2000 and the events taking place at that time.

It may be argued that Satan knows that these are the last days and that he is preparing his people for the events that lie just ahead. But there is a major leap of logic here. It might seem to make sense that Satan has higher knowledge of the timing of the end than we do. The biblical reality is, however, that *Satan has no control over the events and the timing of the End* (Acts 1:6-7). Satan's opinion about just where we are in earth's history is pure speculation. Final events will take place according to God's plans, purposes and timetable (Rev. 17:17). God, and God alone, is in control of these events. God, and God alone, knows when they will take place (Matt. 24:36).

If the angels of heaven don't know when the final events on earth will occur, why would God reveal it to Satan's angels on earth? Even the timing and the reality of the final Satanic deceptions of earth's history are not under Satan's control. God works through them as well to serve His own purposes (2 Thess. 2:9,11). The "prophecies of Mary" are certainly interesting, but they tell us nothing about God's plans and purposes. We have all the information that truly matters in the Bible. Speculating about the devil's plans and purposes only distracts us from the all-important and time-consuming work of understanding and obeying the Scriptures.

I would be genuinely interested to know just when Jesus is going to come. But it is a piece of information that is not worth losing your mind to obtain. Spiritual survival in the last days of earth's history depends on knowing and obeying God's word; leaps of logic will not protect us then.

THE STATEMENTS OF SCRIPTURE

A second reason that I have serious concerns about end-time calculations is the clear statements of Scripture on the subject. We are not the first generation to ask whether the exciting events happening around us might be portents of the impending end of history. Jesus Himself was approached with similar questions, and His answers ought to be of particular interest to us.

Perhaps the most direct parallel to our topic is found in Acts 1:6-7. There the disciples approach Jesus on the very issue of the timing of the End. Notice verse 6:

> So when they met together,
> they asked him,
> "Lord, are you at this time
> going to restore the kingdom to Israel?"

In verse 5 Jesus had promised that the disciples would be baptized with the Holy Spirit in a few days, right there in Jerusalem. This reminded them not only of an earlier prediction of John the Baptist (Matt. 3:11), but also of Old Testament prophecies like Joel 2:28-32 and Isaiah 4:2-6 which foresaw a mighty outpouring of the Spirit in Jerusalem at the End time, the time when God would destroy the enemies of Israel and build His great eschatological kingdom. The disciples were asking Him in a sense, "Have we come to the time when the world as we know it will come to an end, and your eternal kingdom is going to appear?" This is essentially the same question many are asking today in other words. "Are we there yet?" Notice how Jesus responded, according to verse 7:

> *It is not for you to know*
>> the times or dates
>> the Father has set
>> by His own authority.

Jesus doesn't say, "We're not there yet, wait for a few more signs." He basically says, "Wrong question! The timing of the End is none of your business. The Father knows. But it's not for you to know the times or dates." Why? Because it wouldn't be *good* for us to know.

Setting a date for the End that is too far in the future can cause us to put off our preparation. It's not good for us to know. And if a date we have believed in comes and passes, it's not good for us to have believed in a false date either. It is easy to become confused and cynical about the whole matter of faith in God and in His Word. So Jesus says that the times and the seasons of His coming are best left under the control of His Father.

Amazingly, knowledge of the timing of the end is so tightly sealed ("top secret," "known only at the highest level of security clearance") that the earthly Jesus Himself denies knowledge of it, at least in His earthly humanity:

> No one knows about that day or hour,
>> not even the angels in heaven,

nor the Son,
but only the Father.

Matt. 24:36

In light of this reality, it would seem amazing for any other human being to claim knowledge about the timing of the End. The New Testament is clear that Jesus and His disciples spoke of the End as being near. But there is not one word of speculation regarding the timing of the End. Christians were to be prepared for the End without speculating just when that End would come.[6] The New Testament combines the theme of nearness (Matt. 10:23; 16:28; Rev. 1:3; 22:10,12) with the theme of uncertainty (Matt. 24:42-44, 50; 25:13; Mark 13:32-33, 36; Luke 12:35-46).

THE WARNINGS OF ELLEN WHITE

For Seventh-day Adventists there is an unmistakably clear basis for rejecting any attempts to calculate the time of the End. The Spirit of Prophecy writings deal with this issue in a manner that is so breathtakingly clear that one wonders how anyone could possibly think to set any kind of dates (or whatever else they want to call it) within an Adventist context. But we must never underestimate the God-given creativity of human beings. Even when Ellen White was alive, some had the temerity to send her lists of quotations from her own writings to prove that something else she had said was wrong! So there is no end to the power of a passionate idea to overrule any amount of clarity someone else could possibly muster. Ideas can become so powerful that no amount of evidence can break through. Nevertheless, in what follows I will try.

I'd like to begin with *Selected Messages*, book 1, page 188 (the emphasis in these quotes is mine):

It [truth] will **never develop** in any line that will lead us to imagine that we may know the times and the seasons which the Father hath put in His own power. Again and again have I been warned in regard to time setting. **There will never again be a**

message for the people of God that will be based on time. We are not to know the definite time either for the outpouring of the Holy Spirit or for the coming of Christ.

In this statement Ellen White does not just rule out time calculation for her time, she rules it out also for the future. "[Truth] will *never* develop" in a way that enables us to know that which the Father has put in His own power (note the allusion to Acts 1:6-7, which we just looked at). What has the Father put in His own power? The timing of the End. "Again and again have I been warned in regard to time setting." "There will *never again* be a message for the people of God that will be based upon time."

How much clearer can you get? She is not only ruling out setting a date for the Second Coming (which most people have learned to avoid), she is also ruling out all other calculations concerning the End, such as the time when the Holy Spirit will be poured out. So even when people seek to time the Sunday law or aspects of End-time persecution they may not be transgressing the exact letter of her prohibitions, but they are certainly ignoring the clear spirit: "never again a message based on time."

She is even clearer and more specific in *Selected Messages*, book 1, page 189:

We are not to live upon time excitement. . . . **No one will be able to predict** just when that time will come. . . . You **will not be able** to say that He will come **in one, two, or five years**, neither are you to put off his coming by stating that it may not be **for ten or twenty years.**

Once again she rules out not only her present but the future as well. "No one *will be able* to predict. . . ." "You *will not be able* to say. . . ." She goes so far as to specifically rule out our ability to say that Jesus will come in one, two, or five years. If we cannot say that He will come in one, two, or five years, then there is not much value in making any specific comments about the timing of the End. So this statement categorically denies both the value and the possibility of an unequivocal sense that this is truly the End. It also offers a balancing side to this matter. While it is unwise to set dates, it is equally unwise to put off the Lord's coming to a much later time. More on this later.[7]

Selected Messages, book 2, page 84:

> There will **always be** false and fanatical movements made by persons in the church who claim to be led of God—those who will run before they are sent and will give **day and date for the occurrence of unfulfilled prophecy.** The enemy is pleased to have them do this, for their successive failures and leading into false lines cause **confusion and unbelief.**

I realize in writing this book that nothing I say can bring speculation to a halt. There will always be those who claim to be led of God in their unwarranted speculations. Why? Because sensationalism gathers an audience. Sensationalism sells books. Sensationalism pays the bills. Nothing anyone can do will put an end to it. The only purpose for writing about this is to caution as many as are willing to listen. Speculative teachers will always be with us; the purpose of this book is to caution those who would otherwise be influenced by their teachings.

Notice in the above statement that Ellen White not only rules out dating the Second Coming, here she extends her caution to *any unfulfilled prophecy.* No matter what the event and no matter what the prophecy, there will never again be a message for the people of God that is based on time. I honestly don't know how she could have made it any clearer.

Why has God withheld information about the timing of the End from us? Why are there to be no more messages based on time? Because the successive failures of time calculations bring in confusion and unbelief. This point is extremely important. While speculation is usually financially profitable there is a higher motive for calculating the nearness of the End. It is to wake up a sleeping people. It is to get people ready to meet Jesus. This is a high and worthy motive. The problem is that when time moves on, and so far it always has, the results are the opposite of the intention. Instead of positive wakefulness there is confusion. Instead of readiness there is cynicism ("The thing seemed so biblical, maybe I can't trust what anyone says about the Bible, maybe I can't even trust the Bible anymore, maybe I shouldn't listen to any more sermons on the Second Coming"). The motive may be pure, but the results are the opposite of the intention.

In the course of her prophetic ministry, Ellen White made dozens of statements regarding the timing of the End, of which these are but a sampling.[8] Throughout her life and ministry there is a consistent message never to set time in any form. Any attempt to specify the timing of the End or any particular event preceding it is contrary to the clear teaching of the Spirit of Prophecy. If she has not spoken with clarity on this subject, I'm not sure anything in her writings can be considered clear.

THE LESSON OF SDA HISTORY

In my book *What the Bible Says About the End-Time* I describe some twenty Adventist attempts to set dates for the coming of Jesus between 1844 and 1964. Let me share just a few examples here: a more complete account is available in that earlier volume.

After the great disappointment of October 22, 1844, one of our Adventist pioneers, James White, did a lot of thinking. And he thought, "Perhaps the *Day* of Atonement is really the *year* of Atonement." If so, then Jesus would come on the Day of Atonement in 1845. This was certainly very logical from White's perspective. It even seemed to be based on biblical grounds. If I had been there in 1844, I'm pretty sure I would have found it convincing. But it was wrong.

Early Seventh-day Adventists thought of themselves as modern Israel making their way through the wilderness into the promised land.[9] It was natural that some might suggest that the forty years of Israel's wandering in the desert would be duplicated spiritually in their experience, especially since Ellen White often made that connection. They also noted the text, "This generation will certainly not pass away until all these things have happened" (Matt. 24:34 NIV). Thus attention focused on the year 1884. Again it appeared logical and biblical. Again I probably would have taken it seriously had I been alive then. Again the emphasis was wrong even though seemingly based on the Bible and the Spirit of Prophecy.

In the years after 1888 there was a great revival of the gospel among

Seventh-day Adventists. This revival came at the same time that a Senator named Blair introduced a bill in the United States Senate that would have established a national Sunday law. The existence of a major revival combined with the specter of a National Sunday Law convinced many Adventists that the End was at hand. While there was no direct biblical basis for this timing, current events certainly seemed compelling. I suspect that I, too, would have been moved by the power of events. But time passed, events moved on, and the excitement again proved mistaken.

World War I came around. In the year 1917 the Turks and the British fought a battle in the valley of Megiddo. And many, including some fine evangelists, preached that this battle must be related to the battle of Armageddon; the Lord was about to come. Baptisms in that year were triple what they were before and after. But, as the battle of Megiddo passed and time went on, the fervor of the moment again proved mistaken.

Back in the 1950s I remember people talking about the Bible text, "As it was in the days of Noah, so it will be at the coming of the Son of Man " (Matt. 24:37, NIV). Since Adventists believed that the year 1844 ushered us into the Time of the End, it was suggested that if the End time was as long as the days of Noah (who preached for 120 years), Jesus would come in 1964, and history as we know it would come to an end. How could I argue the point? The date 1964 was based on a logical analogy and a Bible text. It seemed reasonable. It seemed biblical. Yet once again the calculations were wrong.

History has not been kind to date-setters, neither those who have proclaimed an exact date, nor those who sought merely to proclaim the absolute nearness of the End at a particular time and place. Perhaps someday someone will be right about the timing of the End, but it will probably be for the wrong reason. *The lesson of Adventist history is that the very process of calculating the End is flawed.* When a new scheme comes along, no matter how convincing, we must never forget that *those who do not learn from the mistakes of the past are forced to repeat them.*

Nothing has changed. I recently learned the mathematical fact that 666 times 3 equals 1998. Now there is a certain symmetry there, but if you are reading this book, you know that history was not kind to that insight either.

The problem with attempts to calculate the timing of the End is that it is usually impossible to prove them right or wrong until the time passes. They have a certain logic about them (with leaps often well disguised). They often appear to have a biblical basis. They may come from people of high spiritual character and reputation. They may be given with the highest purity of intentions. And before the time passes, it may be impossible to prove that the conclusion is wrong. So the evocative power of time calculation will probably be with us until the End itself.

As a Seventh-day Adventist, however, there are two things about this history that I find very encouraging. For one, it shows that Adventists care about the coming of Christ. It matters to us how long we must wait. The second encouraging point is this: *The Seventh-day Adventist Church as a body has never set or endorsed a date for the second coming of Christ.* It is interesting that many of the people who are now setting dates feel that the General Conference is in apostasy. But on this particular issue, history shows us that the leadership of the church has always been on the right side, and the dissidents have always been on the wrong side.

THE EXAMPLE OF THE FIRST COMING

There is one final reason to question any attempt to discern the timing of the End. This is not a new thing. There is no question that discerning the timing of the End was a very popular thing to do back in Jesus' day. There is a whole category of ancient literature known as Apocalyptic.[10] Covering the period before, during, and just after the writing of the New Testament, attempts were made to outline the events leading up to the End, and to calculate the time when the Messiah would arrive. Current events and prophetic sequences were of major interest. You could say that they had developed detailed prophetic charts for the purpose of getting a clear handle on the future.

At least one major branch of Jewish Apocalyptic, the one most compatible with Pharisaism,[11] depicted a spectacular climax to human history with the arrival of the Messiah.[12] The coming of the Messiah would be accompanied by great signs, followed by the end of human history, which would return the world to its pre-creation condition. After this, the world would be restored, the final judgment would take place, and eternal righteousness would reign.[13] While this picture is not all that different from what we find in the book of Revelation, it is quite different from the visible realities of Jesus' first advent. Is it any wonder, given the spectacular nature of apocalyptic expectation, that Jesus' messianic claims were rejected by many?

Here is an amazing thing. Some of the very people who invested the most time in the study of prophecy ended up missing the real thing when it came. Like Saul of Tarsus, many rejected Jesus because His life and teaching did not conform to their apocalyptic expectations.[14] In their apocalyptic calculations, they went beyond the evidence and purpose of Scripture, seeking information that God had not intended them to have. In the process they unfitted themselves for the task of recognizing the Messiah when He came. The very ones who had carefully worked out the details of God's future work ended up rejecting that same work when it appeared to them.

One way to be unprepared for the work of God in the future is to neglect the study of prophecy. But another way to be unprepared is through the attempt to know more about the future than the prophecies were intended to deliver. You see, the primary purpose of prophecy is not to satisfy our curiosity about the future; it is to help us to recognize the work of God *when* it occurs. Note the statement of Jesus in John 14:29 (and 13:19):

> I have told you now before it happens,
> So that when it does happen you will believe.

The lesson here is that time calculation, apocalyptic expectation, and current-events speculation can cause us to repudiate the actual work of God when it occurs because it doesn't fit our "scriptural" understanding. It is very important that we study the Bible carefully in order to understand prophecy.[15] But it is dangerous to be more specific about the future than Scripture is. God retains the freedom to surprise us, as the first advent of Christ surprised apocalyptic thinkers in the first century. The events of Christ's first advent set a pattern for how we should look forward to the Second Coming.

We must be careful that our excitement over the times in which we live does not tempt us to think we can know that which only God knows. We need to know what the Scriptures teach, but we must be careful not to go beyond what the Scriptures say. Some will fail to be ready for the Second Coming because they are spiritually asleep. But the pattern of the first century tells us that others will fail to be ready because the final events do not conform to their detailed expectations.

CONCLUSION

In this chapter I offer five reasons to be cautious about voices suggesting that the arrival of a new millennium will usher in the final conclusion of all things. I most certainly hope that they are right, even if for the wrong reason. But in spite of the unusual events of the last decade, and also of the year or two just ahead as I write, the current round of calculation and current-events speculation is no more conclusive than previous attempts.

So what shall we do with the year 2000, then? Could it really be that such a magical number has *no* eternal significance? Could it really be that all the exciting events we are experiencing are just the prelude to another decade, another century, even another millennium of the same? How would God want us to approach the days just ahead, no matter the outcome?

In the next chapter I review the greatest precedent to our current situation, the year 1000. What actually happened on that date? What similarities are there to our current situation? What can we learn, if anything, from the aftermath? The answers that I share with you in the next chapter were a surprise to me as I discovered them.

---

1. For example, inflation is measured and fueled by the rising values of land and other fixed properties in today's world. But if property always returned to the original owners every fifty years, land values would never inflate, they would actually diminish with time as the date of the Jubilee approached. Land would be valued in terms of the years of production that remained before the Jubilee (Lev. 25:27-28). This principle would provide a major barrier against inflation. The Jubilee also insured that no family would be permanently impoverished by the financial irresponsibility of an earlier generation.
2. They may have an impact on the theology of the Second Coming, but there is no evidence tying them to the timing of the Second Coming.

3. "This mystery has been revealed . . . so that you, O king, may know the interpretation and that you may understand. . . . You are that head of gold. After you, another kingdom will rise. . . . The great God has shown the king what will take place in the future." Dan. 2:30, 38, 39, 45 (NIV).

4. If anyone can demonstrate from clear texts of Scripture that this principle (that explanations are always in terms of the prophet's point of view) is incorrect, I am open to correction. But from my study of the Bible it seems too clear that God always meets people where they are, that revelation always comes in the time, place, language, and circumstances of the prophet. To abandon this principle opens scriptural interpretation to endless fantasy.

If the seven kings of Revelation 17 represent kingdoms, the five fallen ones are probably the five major Old Testament oppressors of Israel, Egypt, Assyria, Babylon, Medo-Persia, and Greece. John's contemporary would be the pagan Roman Empire, the seventh would be papal Rome in the Middle Ages. The eighth would be the End-time coalition of Revelation 17, coming in the spirit and the power of one of the earlier seven (Babylon, pagan Rome, papal Rome?). See Rev. 17:9-11.

5. Moore provides a discussion of this point in *The Coming Great Calamity*, pp. 97-106.

6. Kyle, p. 33.

7. See chapter 6 for a more extensive discussion of how to balance anticipation of the End with sober attention to the ongoing realities of life.

8. There are two major published collections of Ellen White's comments in regard to date setting and speculation regarding the End. They are found in *Selected Messages*, book 1, pp. 185-192 and in the new compilation called *Last Day Events*, pp. 32-42. I challenge skeptical readers to not just read the compilations, but to read each of these statements in its original context so that my brevity in this context cannot be misunderstood.

9. Taylor Grant Bunch, "The Exodus and Advent Movement in Type and Antitype," mimeographed transcript of 36 sermons delivered during the Sabbath afternoon vespers services in the Battle Creek Tabernacle, 1937.

10. For a standard scholarly treatment of Apocalyptic literature see D. S. Russell, *The Method and Message of Jewish Apocalyptic* (Philadelphia: Westminster Press, 1964). An excellent, brief summary can be found in Paul D. Hanson, "Apocalypses and Apocalypticism," in *The Anchor Bible Dictionary* (N.Y.: Doubleday, 1992), vol. 1, pp. 278-282. The major apocalyptic texts can be read in English translation in the work of James H. Charlesworth, editor, *The Old Testament Pseudepigrapha* (Garden City, N.Y.: Doubleday, 1983), vol. 1, pp. 3-770.

11. Hanson, p. 281.

12. And in one case even the death of the Messiah, cf. 4 Ezra 7:26-34.

13. For a more detailed discussion of Jewish Apocalyptic and its impact on Paul, both before and after he became a follower of Jesus see Jon Paulien, *What the Bible Says About the End-Time* (Hagerstown, Md.: Review and Herald Publishing Association, 1994), pp. 65-71, 76-77.

14. Note Ellen White's comments on this very point in *Desire of Ages*, pp. 29-30.

15. My primary purpose in the earlier book, *What the Bible Says about the End-Time*, was to lay out the kind of big-picture perspective that would help people discern not only what the Bible actually says about the End, but also what it doesn't say. If that book gives the correct picture, we have a basic picture of the kinds of events that will accompany the End, events that are unprecedented in human history.

The Year 1000:
Is It Deja Vu All Over Again?

There is a great deal of confusion these days as to whether the year 1000 provides a helpful analogy to what we are experiencing as we approach the year 2000. Was there a great deal of excitement in Europe as the year 1000 approached? Or is this something we project back to that time because of our own expectations for the year 2000? What lessons do the events surrounding the year 1000 offer for us today? We will begin the chapter by looking at the year 1000 from the perspective of popular imagination.

THE YEAR 1000 IN POPULAR IMAGINATION

It was the close of the year 999. The long-awaited end of the millennium was at hand. The people of Europe gathered in panic-stricken groups to await the catastrophic conclusion of all things. Throughout the year portents of the End, such as the birth of two-headed calves, seemed to be everywhere. When men and women looked up they saw the bright tails of comets at night and terrifying shapes in the clouds by day. A series of solar and lunar eclipses not only darkened the earth; they darkened the minds of the people with foreboding.

In preparation for the End, the wealthy donated lands and other property to the Church and headed for Jerusalem or monasteries. Merchants closed up shop and distributed their money to the poor. Rich men surrendered wagon-loads of jewels in the hope that Christ would find them in a state of grace when the End came. Peasants abandoned their crops and herds and journeyed to see the latest relics. Debts were forgiven, convicts were released from prison, husbands and wives forgave each other their infidelities.

As the dawn of the new year approached, the portents increased. There were monstrous downpours of rain, whole villages were swallowed up by earthquakes and flood, other parts of the countryside were ravaged by drought and famine, and the cities of Europe were devastated by outbreaks of the plague. Large buildings collapsed suddenly, as if moved by unseen hands. Wandering hermits delivered impassioned sermons about the need for repentance in the few days remaining before the final judgment. A wave of suicides swept over the continent as people buckled under the pressure of the impending apocalypse. In Rome a new pope of a different order was placed on the throne. Sylvester II was an astrologer and a wizard who openly participated in spiritualistic rituals. It is, therefore, not surprising that whispers of Antichrist circulated among the people at his coronation and afterward.

On New Year's Eve of December 31, 999, churches and chapels everywhere were filled with Christian penitents awaiting with utmost anxiety whatever the darkness would bring forth at the stroke of midnight. The suspense of that hour united all of European Christianity into a single community of faith and fear. Families gathered their loved ones about them and looked up into the heavens in expectation.

When nothing in particular happened that night, history, society, and geography all entered the year 1000 intact. The bells of churches rang in the second Christian millennium to the sound of hallelujah choruses and prayers of rejoicing. People seized their second probation with vigor, revitalizing society and bringing the "dark ages" to an end. Churches were repaired, fields and farms received renewed attention, and merchants set about to do their part in bringing about a golden age of blessing and prosperity on earth. Reborn, European society grew and expanded, unfurling Crusader flags to march out and reclaim Jerusalem from the heathen. While the year 1000 did not turn out to be the opening of an age of terrors, as had been expected, it truly ushered in an age of miracles. It was a year to remember.[1]

HISTORIANS AND THE YEAR 1000

The preceding account is widely circulated and makes sense in the context of popular conceptions of the "Dark Ages." If you examine the consensus of historical scholarship over the last hundred years or so, however, everything you just read about the year 999 *never happened.* Not one bit. Zero. Nichts. Nada. And there is plenty of evidence to back up the consensus. Or shall we rather say that there is a stunning lack of evidence for panic terror, or any unusual level of suicides, forgiveness, divesting of wealth, or even a great deal of awareness that the year 1000 was approaching. More than a score of medieval historians have published books and articles demolishing the evidence for year 1000 excitement.[2] They trace the modern origins of the legend not to original documents of the time but to speculations developed in the sixteenth and seventeenth centuries. These speculations received the aura of established fact when they were uncritically highlighted by certain French historians in the nineteenth and twentieth centuries.[3]

To be totally honest, the scholarly reluctance to attribute significance to the year 1000 is based on more than just a lack of solid evidence. When you know something about reckoning of time in the Middle Ages, the legend of year 1000 excitement doesn't really make a lot of sense. For one thing, as impressive as the round numbers of the decimal system are to us, they had no such hold on the minds of people in the Middle Ages. Roman numerals were still largely in use and as far as we know there was no particular significance attached to the number represented by "M".[4]

Furthermore, we take our system of A.D. dating for granted. But in actual fact, the system hasn't been around forever. In the first several hundred years after the birth of Christ most Europeans either counted their years in terms of the reign of current ruler, the beginning of their ruler's dynasty, or the founding of Rome or the Olympic Games.[5] Christians (as did the Jews also) tended to prefer counting their years from the presumed date of Creation (*Anno Mundi*). There was, however, a considerable variety of opinion as to just when that was, so various segments of the church were on different calendars.[6]

As far as we know, the first date ever based on the year of Christ's birth (*Anno Domini*) was the year A.D. 526. A Scythian monk, Dionysius Exiguus (Dennis the Small, sometimes spelled Exiguous) sought to unite the calendars of Christendom. Instead of dates dependent on the vagaries of Old Testament chronology, or on the games and rulers of a fallen empire, he chose to base his calendar on the birth of Jesus. Utilizing the evidence available to him, he calculated that Jesus was born just before the end of year 753, according to the founding of Rome calendar. Year 754 on that calendar became year 1 of his *Anno Domini* calendar. (For Dennis, then, Jesus was actually born at the end of "year zero," which only centuries later was finally designated 1 B.C.)[7] Dennis, however, accepted the New Year's Day of the Latin churches, which was not actually based on the birth of Christ (December 25), but on the circumcision (January 1).[8]

In spite of serious effort, however, Dennis miscalculated the actual year of Jesus' birth by about four years, and this error has never been corrected. A.D. 2000, therefore, turns out to be about 2004 years after the events of the nativity.[9] Thus the value people place on the year 2000 is not based on the accuracy of the beginning date, but the perceived religious or political significance of the number itself.

The work of Dionysius was not immediately accepted everywhere. Adopted by the Synod of Whitby in 664, the A.D. system spread slowly from Anglo-Saxon territories of England through the Carolingian domains (in modern-day France) to the rest of Western Europe. Most reluctant of the Western European peoples were those living in the areas known as Spain and Portugal today. These remained loyal to a reckoning based on the Roman conquest of their peninsula. Most Christians further east retained the Byzantine calendar, which was moored to the date of Creation, while the Armenians dated their years from the time of their split from the rest of the church.[10]

So as the year we call 1000 approached there was no uniform system

of counting years in Europe. Any year 1000 excitement would by defini-
tion have to be limited largely to England and France. To make that even
less likely, there seems to have been no unified practice regarding when to
start the new year. In Rome the new year was reckoned from the date of
the Nativity (December 25), but in Florence New Year fell on Annunciation Day (March 25—the date of Jesus' conception). In Venice, New Year
fell on March 1, in England on either Annunciation Day, Christmas, or
January 1, in Spain and Portugal the date was always January 1, in the
Byzantine world it was September 1 or 24 and in Armenia it was July 9.[11]
So not only was there no agreement on what year it was, but there was no
agreement on just when that year began.

Even the start of a New Year's Day was in question. Did it begin at
midnight, with the hour and worship service called *matin*, or did it begin
at dawn, when people headed out to work in the fields, or did it begin at
sundown, according to the practice of Jews and some in the Eastern
Church?[12] When many monarchs still counted years by the time of their
accession, and there was so much confusion as to just when a day and a
year began, is there any reason at all to think that anything special happened at the approach of the year 1000?

To top it all off, among the limited range of documents that survives
from the period just before and after the year 1000, not one makes reference to a widespread panic associated with the date. On the contrary
there is no shortage of deeds and wills, made shortly before 1000, the
provisions of which look well past that year.[13] For example, in 998 the
Council of Rome imposed on the French king Robert a penance of seven
years.[14]

HISTORIANS RETHINK THE YEAR 1000

You would think that evidence like the above would settle the matter,
but in fact the case with regard to year 1000 excitement is not yet closed.
The latest crop of historians has brought fresh insight to our understanding of the end of the first millennium. Hillel Schwartz notes, "Despite
our conservative medievalists with their scrutiny of sources, the millennial
'panic terror' surfaces again and again in the works of prominent modern
historians, literary analysts, cultural critics, political commentators, uni-

versity presidents, novelists, journalists, and futurologists."[15] When so many hold something to be true, it would seem that there *must* be something to it.

Upon further examination of the evidence it appears that apocalyptic thinking was, after all, fairly widespread in the tenth and eleventh centuries (A.D.900-1100), at least in England and France, where the *Anno Domini* dating standard was first accepted.[16] Joseph B. Trahern, Jr., a scholar of Old English Literature, notes a significant passage in the *Blickling Homily XI*:

> Nevertheless, we know that it is not far off, because all the signs and fore-tokens that our Lord previously said would come before Doomsday, are all gone by, except one alone, that is, the accursed stranger, Antichrist, who, as yet, has not come hither upon earth. Yet the time is not far distant when that shall also come to pass; because this earth must of necessity come to an end in this age which is now present, for five of the [fore-tokens] have come to pass in this age; wherefore this world must come to an end, and of this the greatest portion has elapsed, even nine hundred and seventy-one years, in this year.[17]

Likewise, around the year 1000 itself the two great prose writers of the late Old English period, Aelfric and Wulfstan, both expressed their conviction that "the ending of this world" was approaching in haste.[18]

There are similar witnesses to the situation in France at the time. In 998 Abbon of Fleury wrote how he, as a youth, heard a preacher in Paris announcing the end of the world for the year 1000, to be followed shortly by the Last Judgment.[19] In 960 Bernard, a well-known hermit in Thuringia announced that God had revealed to him the imminent end of the world.[20] Abbon also wrote about battling year 1000 excitement in Lorraine in the 970s.[21] But the best-known apologist for the first millennium was the monk Raoul Glaber, who wrote from about 1025 to 1030. He considered the year 1000 from "the birth of the Word" (the Nativity)[22] to be an extremely significant year. He saw signs in his own experience of the unleashing of Satan at the end of the millennium.[23] But since the world had not come to an end in the thousandth year after the Nativity, he focused his attention on the year 1000 after the Passion, the Cross and the Resurrection, which by his reckoning was the year 1033.[24] That year witnessed a strange solar eclipse, reported to have created a "sapphire mist," and an earthquake that shook the Holy Land. The year was preceded by storms, plagues, famines, and the highest floods in memory.[25] Thus fear seems to have swung from one date to another, depending on the beginning point from which the millennium was computed.[26]

The period marked by the turn of the first millennium in our terms became like the bridge between two ages, dividing and connecting the early and late Middle Ages. There were profound changes in every aspect of Medieval social and cultural life.[27] There was a revival of ancient Roman learning.[28] The period witnessed the birth of knighthood, an attempt to civilize the art of war and bring a greater degree of stability to the lives of the common people.[29] It saw the crowning of Otto III in 996, who dreamed of working with his mentor, who became Pope Sylvester II, to re-establish the glories of Charlemagne and even the Christian Roman Empire of the days of Constantine.[30] It saw the conversion of the Magyars, Poland, Russia and all of Scandinavia.[31] Soon to come were the Crusades, which sought to re-Christianize not only the Bible lands, but also Muslim and Jewish enclaves within Europe itself.

But French historian Henri Focillon notes an amazing paradox: there is abundant evidence of belief in the imminent end of the world in the middle of the tenth century (around A.D. 950) and the first third of the eleventh (A.D. 1000-1033. and beyond), but for the years immediately preceding the year 1000 and for that year itself, we have none.[32] The existence of at least some terror at the time is clear, but its absence in the immediate vicinity of the year 1000 is quite surprising.[33] Even Glaber, who stokes his work with all the fearful portents he can dig up, records nothing particularly startling for the actual year 1000 itself.[34] The best evidence seems to suggest that fear of the approaching end is a constant in the two centuries that sandwich the year 1000, coming to the surface in any crisis, but it does not appear to be generally attached to three zeros on a calendar.

The period surrounding our year 1000, then, appears to have been a fairly significant time in history, a time of great changes and considerable anxiety. But the excitement in the end seems to have had relatively little to do with the numbering of years and a whole lot more to do with the religious and social changes that were taking place at that time.[35] In the words of Bernard McGinn:

> Exaggerated emphasis on the turn of the millennium, or indeed any specific date in the list of the many at some time identified with the end during the five centuries between 1000 and 1500, tends to minimize the pervasiveness of apocalypticism throughout these centuries. Medieval folk lived in a more or less constant state of apocalyptic expectation difficult to understand for most of us today.[36]

The experience of Europe a thousand years ago, therefore, even that of England and France where the greatest opportunity for year 1000 excitement existed, provides less of a precedent for our own situation than we might have expected.[37]

CENTURY'S END

If there is so little concrete evidence for a great excitement around the year 1000, then, why have people been so sure for so long that there will be some special kind of excitement as we approach the year 2000? Historian Hillel Schwartz develops the compelling thesis that the year 2000 is climax of a series of end-of-century fixations that have occurred over the last seven hundred years.[38] To use Schwartz's own words:

> If [end-of-century excitement] is a trick, it is a trick that in the West has been played at least seven times before, a trick that works because we are time-minded enough to prospect for ends, numerate but visionary enough to be impressed by imaginary numbers, punctual enough to attend to a common calendar of years. . . . Our cultural inheritance of [end of century] experiences has set us up to expect the end of a century to be the end of an era, the new century to initiate a new age. We may not hurry

into white gowns or gather on hilltops, but at each century's end, the X's on the calendar do seem darker, do seem to be leading us beyond the run-of-the-mill toward apocalypse.[39]

Schwartz notes that the 1290s marked the first end of a Christian century that was truly celebrated by Christians as a century's end.[40] All the ingredients for an end of century focus were in place. Most of Europe finally had a standard calendar (*Anno Domini*), an arithmetic sense of the passage of time, a concern with ages and periods, a sense of the decay of institutions and the approach of the last days, and the prophetic hope of a new, reformed age within history. Over subsequent centuries the standard calendar became more universal and anticipation of the end of century more pronounced. But there is reasonably secure evidence that the 1290s witnessed the first major recognition of a century's end.[41]

In the sixteenth century Nostradamus, a French physician and chef of Jewish heritage, but born to a father forced to convert to Catholicism around 1501, became renowned on account of predictions that seemed to come true a short time after they were made. Emboldened by his success at predicting the near future, Nostradamus tried his hand at predicting major events over the following two thousand years or so.[42] He laid out his predictions in a thousand four-line poems or quatrains, divided into 'centuries' of a hundred each. Many of his predictions were even attached to specific dates.[43]

The point of Schwartz's reference to Nostradamus is the fixation on centuries as a point of reference. Not only does Nostradamus divide his work into "centuries" but the specific dates that he chooses to mention tend to focus on the ends and beginning of centuries, as is the case with his "prediction" for the year 1999. A careful analysis of events at the close of centuries since the year 1300 substantiates Schwartz's case that there has been increasing attention to the end of each century.[44] The concept seems to be building toward a climax in our time.

Each century's end since the year 1300 has borne ever more vivid witness to the ambivalence inherent in Western millennial visions of decay and disaster aforehand, re-creation and regenera-

tion 'in the sweet bye and bye.' Nightmares unconfirmed, uto-
pian dreams unfulfilled, these do not fade forever from memory
as a new century goes resolutely on. Prophecies unachieved in
past '99s, '00s, '01s tend to accumulate toward successive centuries' ends. However disturbing it may seem to the historian accustomed to careful alignment of events in patient sequence, the jumps
from one *fin de siècle* [French for 'end of century'] to the next have
become cumulative, . . . building—as the prophecies themselves
have built—toward the end of the 20th century.[45]

Since the twentieth century bears the same relation to the next millennium as the nineties bear to each new century, the tension related to
every end of century has to a degree applied to the entire twentieth century. And what a century it has been! The greatest wars in history have
been fought within our lifetime. The most sophisticated and gruesome
attempts to destroy whole peoples have occurred within our lifetimes
Transportation in this century has moved from horse and buggy to cars,
airplanes, and space shuttles. Communication has advanced from tele-
graph and telephone to two-way video and instant transmission of knowledge to every corner of the globe. Knowledge itself is doubling every few
years, even as the tools for managing that knowledge explode in power
and sophistication. Science probes the far limits of the universe, provides
the tools for an unprecedented level of human comfort, and at the same
time dispenses the means to forever destroy life on this planet.

That we assume the year 1000 was a significant year may tell as much
about the year 2000 as anything that actually happened back then. Our
corporate concern with history and the meaning of time is about to col-
lide with the fortuitous occurrence of a magical number, whose symbolic
power has grown with each passing century. We have learned to use the
ends of centuries not only to mark history but prophecy as well. "There's
something exhilarating about believing that you live at the turning point
in human and cosmic history, that God has somehow chosen you to be a
key player in the ultimate resolutions of good and evil".[46] The entire world,
Muslim and Jew, Catholic, Orthodox, and Protestant, secular and religious, socialist and capitalist, from Wall Street economist to tribal patri-

arch, now regulates its life in terms of the Dionysius calendar. For the first time, the entire world will share a synchronous experience of century's end.[47] One observer has likened this experience to "a period of mass reflection—as if the whole world were turning 40 simultaneously."[48]

Popular media, from movies to television to music to journalism, all exude the sense that we are living in special times. For the first time in history the end of the world is seen as something that could come, not at the hands of an angry God, but at the blundering hands of science and technology. For the first time we are capable of ending our own world without outside help. This year has long been a focus of doomsayers and "prophets" like Nostradamus. There is no future date (like 2525, 3000 or 6666) that has quite the "immense historical symbolism and psychological power" of this number.[49] And compounding it all is the sudden appearance of a millennium bug that threatens TEOTWAWKI: The End Of The World As We Know It. The end result is an amazing notion: secular apocalypse.

The millennial year 2000 has been in the popular imagination for a whole century now. The entire century has been perceived as a final epoch, an apocalyptic century.[50] Eschatology, or the study of last things, has moved to the forefront of scholarship in the secular domain as well as the religious. The end of this century has witnessed the transition from the Modern Age to the "post-modern" world, from the industrial age to the information age. And with it all is a world in "future shock,"[51] holding its breath in anticipation of the worst, while at the same time, hoping for the dawning of a new age in which peace and prosperity will become real.[52]

Although there are fewer lessons to be learned from the experience of those who lived in the year 1000 than we might have hoped, an examination of the events of that time and the history leading up to our own time has led us to realize that there is a strong secular swell underlying this fascination with the year 2000.[53] In the words of Daniel Cohen: "Perhaps the year 1000 meant little to men of the Middle Ages, but the year 2000 means a great deal to modern numerologists who believe that there is an overpowering significance to certain numbers and dates."[54]

This leaves Adventist Christians with a profoundly disturbing question. Can we allow the secularists of this world to outpreach us on the

End? Is there ever a time when Adventists should be more cautious than the average person on the street? Is there any Word from the Lord in all of this? Is this a purely secular fascination or is there an inspired basis for seeing special significance in the year 2000?

There is a tradition in Adventism that seems to offer a basis for answering that question in the positive. It is the tradition that the second coming of Jesus will occur around the six thousandth year of earth's history, ushering in a millennial Sabbath in heaven. In the following chapter, I will look at the history of that tradition and examine the Bible and Spirit of Prophecy evidence to see if there is some inspired basis for this expectation.

---

1. It is interesting that an account like this appears in a pair of books published within two years of each other, whose authors both claim to be historians. One mocks the description with delightful tongue-in-cheek humor (Hillel Schwartz, *Century's End: A Cultural History of the Fin de Siècle from the 990s through the 1990s* [New York: Doubleday, 1990], pp. 3-6). The other appears to take it with utmost historical seriousness (Richard Erdoes, *A.D. 1000: Living on the Brink of Apocalypse* [San Francisco: Harper and Row, 1988], pp. 1-9). In spite of the title, Erdoes' work is actually a biography of Gerbert of Aurillac, who became Pope Sylvester II (999-1003 A.D.), pp. vii-xii. See also the account included in Damien Thompson, *The End of Time: Faith and Fear in the Shadow of the Millennium* (Hanover, N.H.: University Press of New England, 1996), pp. 35-37.

2. A list of significant works is given in Schwartz, note 3, pp. 299-300.

3. Joseph B. Trahern, Jr., "Fatalism and the Millennium," in *The Cambridge Companion to Old English Literature*, edited by Malcolm Godden and Michael Lapidge (Cambridge: Cambridge University Press, 1991), p. 167; Jacques Barzun and Henry Graff, *The Modern Researcher* (New York: Harcourt, Brace and Company, 1957), p. 104; Schwartz, p. 6.

4. Barzun and Graff, p. 105.

5. Schwartz, pp. 20-23.

6. Thompson, pp. 28-32; Schwartz, pp. 23-25.

7. Thompson, pp, 32-33; Schwartz, pp. 26-27.

8. December 25, of course, is rather unlikely to have been the actual day when Jesus was born. There is no biblical basis for certainty with regard to the exact day of the nativity, or even the time of year.

9. Note the article by Gerhard Pfandl, "The Year 2000? It's Already A.D. 2002," *Australasian Record*, November 15, 1997, pp. 8-9.

10. Summarized in Barzun and Graff, p. 105; Schwartz, pp. 27-28.

11. Schwartz, p. 28.

12. Ibid.

13. Thompson, p. 37.

14. Marjorie Reeves, "The Development of Apocalyptic Thought: Medieval Attitudes," in *The Apocalypse in English Renaissance Thought and Literature*, edited by C. A. Patrides and Joseph Wittreich (Ithaca, N.Y.: Cornell University Press, 1984), p. 46 and reference on p. 67.

15. Schwartz, pp. 7-8.

16. A scholar of old English literature has unearthed fresh examples of doomsday preaching in the context of the year 1000 in England; see Trahern, pp. 167-168. For a summary of the picture in France, see Reeves, pp. 45-46.

17. Trahern, p. 166.

18. Ibid., p. 168.

19. Henri Focillon, *The Year 1000*, translated by Fred D. Wieck (New York: F. Ungar Publishing Co., 1969), p. 54.

20. Ibid., p. 59.

21. Ibid.

22. Quoted in Schwartz, p. 36.

23. Focillon, p. 65.

24. Ibid., pp. 67-68.

25. Schwartz, pp. 7, 37.

26. Focillon, p. 68.

27. Schwartz, p. 32.

28. Felipe Fernández-Armesto, *Millennium: A History of the Last Thousand Years* (New York: Scribner, 1995), p. 62.

29. Schwartz, p. 33.

30. Fernández-Armesto, p. 62; Focillon, pp. 163-164, 182-183; Erdoes, pp. 177, 185-186. The Holy Roman Empire was actually founded in 962 (Erdoes, p. 59), but the unique synergy of Pope Sylvester II and Otto III around the turn of the first millennium promised great things to come out of this union of German and Italian interests (Erdoes, p. 187).

31. Fernández-Armesto, pp. 60-62; see also Focillon, p. 105, Thompson, p. 41, and Trahern, pp. 166-167.

32. Focillon, pp. 59-60, 62.

33. Ibid., p. 72.

34. Reeves, p. 46.

35. Trahern, p. 167.

36. Bernard McGinn, "Apocalypticism and Church Reform: 1100-1500," in *The Encyclopedia of Apocalypticism*, 3 volumes, edited by Bernard McGinn, John J. Collins, and Stephen J. Stein (New York: Continuum, 1998), 2:74-75.

37. There is an interesting new take on this whole business, however. Respected historian Richard Landes argues that there was in fact a great excitement among the common people around the year 1000, but that both the excitement and the evidence for it was suppressed by religious and secular authorities who sought to defuse the inevitable

apocalypticism that would be associated with such a date. The lack of evidence for year 1000 excitement would, therefore, be a result of something akin to a medieval conspiracy.

Landes challenges the historical consensus by taking Glaber more seriously than others have and noting three other references to the year 1000 that are ambiguous for our purposes, yet do seem to suggest that the year was special to at least a handful of witnesses. Landes also believes that the "Peace of God" movement, a precursor to the popular activity preceding the Crusades, was related to the millennium in the popular imagination. And the actions of Otto III in the year 1000 itself may indicate a belief in the significance of that year. Landes's evidence is summarized in Thompson, pp. 48-53.

Landes notes that two versions of the *Anno Mundi* (from the date of creation) dating system disappear suddenly from the West, just before those systems were due to reach the apocalyptic year 6000 in A.D. 500 and again in A.D. 800. The Catholic Church, based on the anti-apocalyptic theology of Augustine (McGinn, p. 75), was anxious to insure that its calendar would not trigger apocalyptic panic. In fact, the very switch to the *Anno Domini* calendar appears to have occurred in part as a way to avoid the apocalyptic implications of the 6000th year of earth's history. Landes's view is summarized in Thompson, pp. 34, 43-44. A one-paragraph summary by Landes himself is found in an interview entitled "Countdown: Every Thousand Years, It Comes Around Just Like Clockwork. What's the Millennium Likely to Mean?" *People*, 48, no. 22, June 9, 1997, pp. 101-103. His evidence is detailed in "Lest the Millennium Be Fulfilled: Apocalyptic Expectations and the Pattern of Western Chronography 100-800 CE," in *The Use and Abuse of Eschatology in the Middle Ages*, edited by Werner Verbeke, Daniel Verhelst and Andries Welkenhuysen (Louvain: Leuven University Press, 1988), pp. 137-211. The evidence is summarized in Thompson, pp,. 48-53. Although Thompson is impressed by Landes's argument and gives much space to it, he seems to feel less than compelled by it in his conclusion (pp. 53-55).

In this chapter I have chosen to highlight only the available evidence and the most logical explanation that can be drawn from that evidence. If Landes should turn out to be correct, the only effect on the thesis of this chapter would be to heighten our awareness of the magical power of numbers in the European mind.

38. For convenience a full reference is given here once more: Hillel Schwartz, *Century's End: A Cultural History of the Fin de Siècle from the 990s Through the 1990s* (New York: Doubleday, 1990). Schwartz's argument is summarized by Thompson, pp. 106-115.

39. Schwartz, p. 9-11.

40. This seems to be confirmed by default in Rosalind Brooke and Christopher Brooke, *Popular Religion in the Middle Ages: Western Europe 1000-1300* (London: Thames and Hudson, 1984, pp. 154-155.

41. Schwartz, p. 55.

42. Ibid., p. 268.

43. Ibid., pp. 99-101. The most famous of Nostradamus's dated predictions today is his prediction for the year 1999 (Schwartz's translation):

> The year 1999, seven months,

> From the sky will come a great King of terror,
> To resuscitate the great king of Angoulmois;
>
> Before, after, Mars will reign by good luck.

This language is clearly ambiguous, but no doubt many will seek to identify its fulfillment in terms of a meteor shower (there is an excellent chance of a major one in November of 1999) and/or any significant conflicts that may break out during the year.

44. Ibid., pp. 17-197.
45. Ibid., p. 11.
46. Landes (interview), *People*, p. 101.
47. Schwartz, p. 275-276.
48. Sarah Ryle, "High anxiety over New Year as Millenium [*sic*] Panic Strikes," posted at reports.guardian.com.uk, October 25, 1998.
49. Kyle, p. 15.
50. Schwartz, p. 239.
51. Alvin Toffler, *Future Shock* (NY, Random House, 1970).
52. Schwartz, p. 264.
53. Landes (interview), *People*, p. 101.
54. Daniel Cohen, *Waiting for the Apocalypse* (Buffalo, NY: Prometheus Books, 1973), p.56.

CHAPTER 5

Adventist Faith and the Year 2000

ADVENTISTS AND THE MILLENNIAL WEEK

Adventist faith did not see any significance in the year 2000 during the last century. There was a clear expectation, however, that the Second Coming would probably occur around the six-thousandth year of earth's history. The millennium, then, would function like a great Sabbath of rest for the earth coming at the conclusion of a great, millennial week of seven thousand years. According to Robert Johnston, all pre-millennialists[1] of the nineteenth century believed in the "cosmic week" of 6000 years of human history followed by a millennial Sabbath.[2] Based on calculations of the date of Creation, therefore, various dates for the second coming of Jesus were set (1866, 1870, 1874, 1881, 1914), particularly in the Jehovah's Witness' tradition.[3]

Our Seventh-day Adventist pioneers inherited the concept of the cosmic or millennial week from William Miller. Miller modified the chronology placed in the margins of the KJV Bible with the result that 1843/44 ended up being the six thousandth year of earth's history, which date appealed to him on many other grounds as well.[4] After the Great Disappointment in 1844, Sylvester Bliss modified the calculations, developing the new understanding that the six-thousandth year of earth's history would be 1882.[5] Articles in the Review and Herald demonstrate this inheritance.[6]

The most influential proponent of the millennial week among nineteenth-century Adventists, however, was John Nevins Andrews, who published a series of six articles in the *Review and Herald* under the general heading of "The Great Week of Time."[7] Andrews felt that the weekly cycle was instituted by God at Creation in order to indicate the period of mankind's probation and judgment.[8] In other words, the weekly cycle is like a parable of the timing of earth's history. For Andrews, the birth of Christ occurred 4115 years after creation.[9] For him, therefore, the sixth thousand years of earth's history began somewhere around A.D. 880 and ended around 1880 or so.[10] While Andrews was very careful not to set an exact date for Jesus' return, he was clearly convinced that "the sixth period of a thousand years must end in this century though we cannot fix the year when it will terminate."[11] Since the six-thousandth year begins the millennium, it is very clear that Andrews anticipated that the second coming of Jesus would occur at the end of 6000 years of earth's history, or sometime shortly after the year 1880.[12]

When the century came to an end without the fulfillment of Andrews' expectation, Uriah Smith, the editor of the *Review*, weighed in forcefully against speculations related to the 6000-year age of the earth.[13] The concept of the millennial week seems to have moved largely into the background for much of the twentieth century until the year 2000 began to approach on the horizon.[14] At that point a familiar feature of the King James Bible began to catch people's attention once more.

THE MILLENNIAL WEEK AND THE YEAR 2000

Adventists raised on the King James Bible (as I was) are generally aware of the dates for biblical events that are often placed in the margin. It doesn't take long for curious readers to go back to Genesis 1 and see what the date for Creation might be. Those who do so find the unequivocal date 4004 B.C. for Creation. If the 4004 date is correct the earth was about 6000 years old sometime in 1996 or 1997. It is not surprising, therefore, that a renewal of the millennial week idea might focus Adventist attention on the years approaching the date A.D. 2000. A brief review of the history of the millennial week may be helpful.

According to Robert Johnston, the millennial-week idea seems to have had its origin among Jewish mystics living about a hundred years before the birth of Christ.[15] While not at first thinking in terms of a seven-thousand year span for human history, the statement in Ps. 90:4, that "a thousand years in thy sight are but as yesterday when it is past," created in the minds of ancient writers the possibility of correlating the weekly cycle with great periods of a thousand years each. In the following centuries a number of rabbis clearly expressed the idea of a millennial week and it was included repeatedly in the Talmud.[16] The same idea is found in Christian writings of the second century, the *Epistle of Barnabas* being the first.[17] Barnabas states, "The Lord will make an end of everything in six thousand years, for a day with him means a thousand years."[18]

Early Christians seem to have followed the evidence in the Septuagint Greek version of the Old Testament, whereas modern translations of the Old Testament are based on the Masoretic Hebrew text. Because the Septuagint text of the Old Testament contains longer periods between birth and fatherhood in the genealogies of Genesis, the period between Creation and the birth of Christ comes out to about 5500 years instead of around 4000. So, early Christians like Barnabas anticipated that history would wind up around A.D. 500.[19] This *Anno Mundi* calendar is still followed in the Eastern Orthodox tradition. In the West, on the other hand, the church switched first to an accounting that put off the End until A.D. 800 and then switched to the *Anno Domini* calendar of Dionysius Exiguus.[20]

In the seventeenth century James Ussher (1581-1656), the Anglican bishop of Armagh in Ireland, set his hand to determine the date of Creation.[21] Guided by the conviction of a 4000-year period from Creation to the time of Jesus (held originally by the rabbis) he developed a detailed chronology of the Old Testament that set the birth of Christ at exactly 4000 years after Creation. Since by his time scholars had set the year of Christ's birth at 4 B.C. (correcting the work of Dionysius), the date of Creation was set at 4004 B.C.[22]

Can Ussher's chronology be proved correct? Does the concept of the millennial week, so widespread in nineteenth-century Adventism, provide an inspired basis for seeing unique significance in the events surrounding the year 2000? At least one current Adventist writer has left that impression on many readers.[23] In words reminiscent of J. N. Andrews, he states, "I believe that the evidence is overwhelming that we are the generation that will see the actual, literal, second coming of Christ in the clouds of heaven."[24] Based on considerable and often massive research he argues that the millennial-week theory is defensible from Scripture and "strongly supported" by Ellen White. He states that while we need to beware of exact time predictions, the coming of Christ "will not be a hundred years from now"; in other words, it will certainly be much sooner.[25]

The author's biblical argument begins by noting that God's mighty acts generally occur at a pre-determined time. The 120 years until the Flood (Gen. 6:3), the 400-year sojourn of Abraham's descendants in Egypt (Gen. 15:13), the 70 years of captivity in Babylon (Jer. 25:11), and the timing of the events surrounding the crucifixion of Jesus (Dan. 9:24-27, at the conclusion of the 70 weeks of years) were all a matter of prophecy at one point and were fulfilled at the exact time predicted.[26] Events in the course of Christian history, such as the beginning of the Time of the End (at the close of the 1260 days in 1798) and the beginning of the pre-advent judgment (at the close of the 2300 days in 1844) were also predicted in Scripture and fulfilled at the appointed time.[27] He concludes, with the apparent support of Ellen White, that the Second Coming will also occur at a fixed and appointed time.[28]

When will that fixed and appointed time come? 6000 years from the date of Creation. How can one figure? "In a nutshell, from Genesis, chapters 1 and 2, one gets the weekly cycle-six days of work and one for rest. From Leviticus, chapter 25, one gets the sabbatical year-six years to work the land and one to let it rest. From 2 Peter, chapter 3, we observe that with the Lord a day is as a thousand years. And from Revelation, chapter 20, we observe that the 'day of the Lord' is one thousand years long."[29] That this evidence leads one to the idea of a millennial week is supported by William Miller, J. N. Andrews, and, the writer asserts, Ellen White.[30]

Crucial to the author's argument is his interpretation of 2 Pet. 3:8:

"With the Lord a day is like a thousand years." "Peter pictured a long delay in Christ's coming (2 Pet. 3:3, 4); he illustrated the delay by the long period from Creation to the Flood (3:5-7); he gave the approximate limits of probationary time by comparing the days of the week with 1,000-year periods (3:8); he gave God's longsuffering as the reason for the delay (3:9)."[31] Since the day referred to in verse 8 is associated with the "day of judgment" (2 Pet. 3:7), the "day of the Lord" (3:10) and the "day of God" (3:12), it must be a reference to the millennium of Revelation 20. *The Day of the Lord, beginning with the Second Coming, will be a thousand years long.* Since the Day of the Lord is associated in the Bible with Sabbath rest, the millennium becomes the capstone to a great week of seven thousand years, with the second coming of Jesus occurring around year 6000 of that great week.[32]

The author then states his understanding that Ellen White believed in the millennial week and clearly taught it in statements such as the following: "For six thousand years the great controversy has been in progress. . . . Now all have made their decisions; the wicked have fully united with Satan in his warfare against God. The time has come for God to vindicate the authority of His downtrodden law."[33]

For the author, the case is settled with this evidence. And who can deny that the thesis is extremely appealing to our own sense of order as well as God's? I am thoroughly attracted to the idea of world history fitting neatly into a package set by the weekly cycle and capped off by a glorious millennial Sabbath. I find the symmetry of it very compelling. But the book unfortunately leaves the impression that time is likely to wind up somewhere in the 90s or shortly thereafter. Since people make life and death decisions on such suggestions, I am compelled to ask a hard and often unpopular question: Is the millennial-week thesis based on the clear and unmistakable teachings of Scripture and the Spirit of Prophecy or could it ultimately be based primarily upon our own human need for order and consistency?

THE BIBLE AND THE MILLENNIAL WEEK

In an earlier chapter I pointed out that attempts to discern the timing of the end, whether specific or general, all require a "leap of logic" if one is to follow the argument to a conclusion. At some crucial point you have to accept a basic assumption or make some kind of intellectual jump, without explicit evidence, in order to reach the desired conclusion.

In what follows I want to make it clear that I respect the scholarship and the Christian integrity of Adventists who believe in the millennial-week theory. And I have gained valuable insights from the writings of the individual whose views I have just shared. Differences on this point are not issues of fellowship. But I believe that the millennial-week theory lacks the clear, inspired support necessary to make it a basis for Christian faith and action. Please note the following points.

1. **There is no explicit statement anywhere in the Bible that connects the coming of Jesus with the six thousandth year of earth's history.** Nor is there any explicit statement that would offer inspired support for the millennial-week theory. The weekly Sabbath is clearly based on the Bible. The seven-year sabbatical cycle is clearly found there also. The Jubilee concept is clearly there. But the idea of a millennial week is never clearly stated and can only be inferred by analogy on the basis of great effort.[34] The millennial-week theory is appealing to the heart and to the human sense of order, but even at its best, as in the case summarized above, it is not based on the clear teachings of Scripture. While one can make a tentative case, based on early Jewish and Christian evidence,[35] that one or more writers of the New Testament may have believed such a concept, a clear, inspired mandate from God is missing.

2. **Nowhere in the Bible is the exact age of the earth stated, nor is it readily calculable from Scripture.** Determining the date of Creation, for example, requires piecing together a number of bits of information in various genealogies and king lists, a process that is vexing at best.[36] This difficulty is compounded by the fact that the three major text traditions of the Old Testament all have different numbers at crucial points.[37] The Hebrew Masoretic text is the basis for both our English Bible translations and for the roughly 4000-year calculations of time from Creation to the birth of Christ. But it was not the Bible used by most New Testament writers and early Christians. That Bible was the Greek translation of the Old Testament known as the Septuagint. Different numbers for the ages of the patriarchs led them to conclude a 5500-year course from Creation

to the Nativity.[38] This calculation was widely accepted by the earliest Christians.[39] So there is no unequivocal biblical or ancient support for a chronology that would bring the earth to its six-thousandth year around A.D. 2000.

Related to this is the problem of Ussher's chronology, the basis for millennial-week theories that point roughly to the year 2000 as the time of the Second Coming. Recent research has demonstrated that while Ussher was a solid scholar in his own right, his own concept of the big picture of human history influenced the details of his chronological work in such a way as to produce the desired conclusion of exactly 4000 years from Creation to the birth of Christ.[40] This is circular reasoning. Based on the evidence, the Bible clearly supports a short chronology for the age of the earth. But the exact age of the earth is neither stated nor calculable on the basis of the Bible.[41]

3. The timing of the End is not given in Bible prophecy. It is true that God often operates on the basis of appointed times which are fulfilled at a specified juncture in history. And there is more than just a hint in Acts 1:7 that there is an appointed time for the Second Coming. In the text Jesus says (my translation from the original), "It is not for you to know the times and the seasons which the Father has appointed by his own authority." If "times and seasons" is Jesus' way of speaking about the timing of the Second Coming (as would seem to be the case on the basis of the question in Acts 1:6),[42] that time is already "appointed" by the Father.

But at the same time, Jesus makes it clear that the exact timing of this appointment is not a subject of prophecy; it is "none of our business." Unlike the timing of the Exodus or the crucifixion, God has not chosen to make the timing of the Second Coming available to the human race in advance. Jesus' statement is in perfect and clear harmony with the testimony of Ellen White. "There will never again be a message for the people of God that will be based on time. We are not to know the definite time either for the outpouring of the Holy Spirit or for the coming of Christ."[43]

One thing is clear, therefore, the validity of the millennial week is at best far from certain. The testimony of Jesus and Ellen White is clear. We will not know the basis of God's "appointment" for sure until it is all over.

Whatever pattern He may choose, we will be satisfied in the end that He chose well. But it is not for our good to know it now.

4. **2 Peter 3 does not speak to the issue**. A crucial linchpin in many arguments for the millennial week is the interpretation of 2 Peter 3.[44] It is argued, for example, that since the day referred to in verse 8 is associated with the "day of judgment" (2 Pet. 3:7), the "day of the Lord" (3:10) and the "day of God" (3:12), it must be a reference to the millennium of Revelation 20. Therefore, *the* Day of the Lord, beginning with the Second Coming, will be a thousand years long.

Here one faces a leap of logic. The text of 2 Pet. 3:8 does *not* say that "The Day of the Lord" is like a thousand years. It merely says (my translation), "one day with the Lord is like a thousand years and a thousand years is like one day." If the author wanted to indicate that he had the millennium in mind he could at least have written "like *the* thousand years." But he did not. Neither did he compare the Day of the Lord with a thousand years. He simply says, "one day (a way of saying any full day in Greek) is like a thousand years with the Lord." In any case, the introductory words of verse 8 formally indicate a fresh line of thought rather than an explanatory footnote to "day of judgment" in verse 7.[45]

The simplest explanation for the wording of this text is that the author is offering two reasons for the "delay" of the Second Coming, which will be a trial for believers and the source of mocking on the part of unbelievers. First, while from a human perspective there may be a delay, there is no delay from God's perspective. God doesn't experience time the way we do (2 Pet. 3:8). Second, God "delays," not because He is careless or powerless (as certain people imagine— 3:3-6), but because He is patient with us and wants to give us adequate time to repent and get ready (3:9).[46] Peter concludes by warning, however, that if our experience of delay causes us to lose our alertness, we will be in danger of turning God's patience into a curse (3:11-13). Instead, our experience of delay should urge us on to get everyone ready so that God does not need to exercise patience anymore.[47]

A Jewish work contemporary with 2 Peter demonstrates that "one day is like a thousand years" (based on Psalm 90:4) need not be intended as a precise chronological concept. In 2 Baruch, as in 2 Peter, the contrast between the endless existence of God and the transience of human life is the basis for God's mercy (2 Baruch 48:18; 2 Pet. 3:9).[48] The crucial passage states, "With you, however, the hours are like times [ages], and the days like generations" (2 Baruch 48:13).[49] The likely concern in 2 Peter, therefore, is not how long the day of judgment is, but to give reasons for its delay. One reason is that God does not experience time the way we do.

It is interesting that in one passage Peter can speak about both hastening and delaying the Second Coming (2 Pet. 3:4, 9, 12). While God may have a fixed appointment in mind, circumstances may alter the case. We can hasten the coming of Jesus, and we can delay it.[50] This concept of hastening and delaying suggests that even if 6000 years were in the plan of God, it might fail on account of us! While God loves to work according to carefully arranged timetables, He is not bound by them. Jesus will come at the best time, when circumstances are right. Although the Second Coming itself is not conditional, the *timing* of that event is conditional! The millennial-week theory, therefore, tells us nothing about the timing of the End.

ELLEN WHITE AND THE MILLENNIAL WEEK

The argument is often made that Ellen White herself was a believer in both the millennial week and in Ussher's chronology, therefore, the millennial-week schema has inspired approval even if the details cannot be worked out for certain from the Bible alone.[51] In the words of one author, the millennial week theory is "defensible from Scripture" and "supported strongly" by the Spirit of Prophecy.[52]

Did Ellen White believe in the millennial week? It is certainly true that she never openly rejected the view and it was held by prominent Adventist leaders in her day.[53] Statements such as *Great Controversy*, p. 659 are certainly compatible with such a view.[54] In this she seems to have common ground with most other Adventists of her time. But did she have some sense of when the 6000 years would be up? Did she support Ussher's chronology with its implication of a conclusion to earth's history around the year 2000?

Ellen White certainly seemed to believe that the earth was about 6000 years old in her day.[55] She also made a number of statements to suggest that the time between Creation and the birth of Christ was about 4000 years.[56] On the surface, the latter statement at least would appear to be a strong endorsement of Ussher's chronology. But the evidence is a bit more complicated than it appears at first.

In a White Estate document file there is a paper by Warren Johns which outlines his examination of all of Ellen White's statements related to the age of the earth.[57] There is an interesting variety in these statements. Sometimes she says *nearly* or *almost* six thousand years old,[58] other times she says *about* six thousand years or simply "for six thousand years,"[59] and still other times she says *more than* six thousand years old.[60] The immediate impression left by this variety of statements is that Ellen White was rather imprecise in her assessment of the exact age of the earth.

Johns, however, disagrees. He examines the origin of each statement. He seeks to disregard reprints and later compilations in order to line up only the original statements in exact order. Having done this he concludes that, rather than being imprecise about the age of the earth, Ellen White was extremely precise and consistent. Based on his research, all of her earlier original statements consistently say "almost" or "about" six thousand years (and their parallel terms). Her last four original statements about the age of the earth, on the other hand, read "more than" or "over" six thousand years. In other words, at the time these last statements were made, the 6000-year period was already in the past.[61] According to Johns, the decisive change between these two sets of statements comes around the year 1885. Before 1885 all statements imply either less than 6000 years or about 6000 years. After 1885 all original statements indicate more than 6000 years. How might she have come to such a conclusion? Johns suggests the possibility that Ellen White was influenced by the chronology of Sylvester Bliss, who terminated the 6000 years in 1882.[62]

But what of her statements about 4000 years from Creation to the birth of Christ? They would certainly imply that the 6000 years would end around A.D. 2000. Johns points out, however, that Ussher's 4000 year figure included a 215-year period of Israelite sojourn in Egypt. While early statements of Ellen White are compatible with that conclusion,[63] after 1891 her statements consistently support a longer period of 400 years in Egypt.[64] If the rest of Ussher's chronology is accepted, this would lengthen the period from Creation to the birth of Christ to about 4200 years. The best explanation of the evidence seems to be that her use of the term 4000 years was a round number, not a precise figure.

Johns's methods and conclusions, however, have been challenged on at least two points by William H. Shea of the Biblical Research Institute at the General Conference.[65] Shea points out that Ellen White doesn't actually change her mind on the length of the sojourn in Egypt, rather she changes her exegesis of Gen 15:13,[66] which talks about the descendants of Abraham being enslaved for 400 years in a country not their own. Her later statements clarify that she consistently believed in a long sojourn of about 400 years in Egypt. Shea agrees with Johns, however, that this view is incompatible with Ussher's chronology.[67]

Shea's challenge to Johns is more serious with regard to the 6000-year statements. He notes that while statements in successive editions of *Great Controversy* may have been taken over from earlier sources, they are not changed in the 1911 edition in spite of careful editing in other parts of the book. If Ellen White truly believed that the earth was more than 6000 years old in 1911, she could easily have modified all or most statements to support that view. She did not. So Shea fails to see the kind of precision in Ellen White's statements that Johns has seen.[68]

Depending on how one reads the evidence there are, therefore, two possibilities. One, according to Johns, there is a distinct pattern to Ellen White's statements related to the age of the earth. In this case she would have been expressing the conviction that the earth was already more than six thousand years old in the nineteenth century. Two, according to Shea, there is no pattern to Ellen White's statements related to the age of the earth. In this case Ellen White's statements are general in nature and not intended to express an exact conviction regarding the age of the earth.

It is not necessary for our purposes to settle this question. If Johns is right, the earth is older than six thousand years already and the millennial-week theory is no longer viable. If Shea is right, Ellen White's statements on the age of the earth are too general in nature to be used to calculate the timing of Christ's return. In either case basing one's use of the millennial-week theory on statements of Ellen White is to go beyond what the evidence allows. While Ellen White may have held one or more opinions about the millennial week in the course of her ministry, the writings she left behind do not offer a divine mandate for that theory.

Those who seek Ellen White's support for the millennial week theory must argue, therefore, in the absence of explicit evidence. And to claim that she would support the use of the millennial week to suggest the timing of Christ's return is to ignore some of the clearest statements in all of her writings. She makes statement after explicit statement such as, "there will never again be a message for the people of God that will be based on time,"[69] "we are not to live upon time excitement,"[70] "there would be no definite time in the message given of God since 1844,"[71] and "the shortness of time . . . is not the great motive."[72] On this matter, as in others, clear statements are always to be preferred over inference and silence.

HOW TO RESPOND TO YEAR 2000 EXCITEMENT?

So if it turns out that there is no explicit biblical or Spirit of Prophecy basis for attaching any special significance to the year 2000, how should Adventists respond when fellow believers express excitement about the possibilities that the date might have some kind of special significance? I would like to suggest three possible responses.

1. **Welcome the excitement.** There is no need to be a spoilsport in this matter. Anything that gets people thinking about spiritual things has great potential for good. Many people find it hard to get motivated toward spiritual effort. While date-based excitement is at best a temporary and suspect motivation, if the year 2000 awakens spiritual interest that was not there before, rejoice and work with it. This could be a golden opportunity to present a healthier view of the gospel to someone genuinely interested in how to get ready for final events. As Paul once suggested, it is a matter of rejoicing whenever the gospel is preached, even if the motives or the approach is a little suspect! (Phil. 1:18).

2. **Subject the evidence presented to careful analysis.** When someone comes to you with a new theory that seems to provide support for a time-based approach to the End, take a careful look at the biblical and Spirit of Prophecy evidence that they present in support of their theory. Make sure that the grounds of their excitement are genuine and solid (see the guidelines under Principle Six in the next chapter). As I have tried to

demonstrate in this book, excitement based on the year 2000 does not pass this test. It requires leaps of logic which fail to compel sober students of inspiration. The material in my previous book, *What the Bible Says About the End-Time* is designed to provide a solid biblical basis for thinking about the End of the world.

3. Reject date setting in all its forms. As noted in the earlier chapters of this book, the Bible, the Spirit of Prophecy, and history are all in agreement that date setting is inappropriate for Christians and has serious spiritual consequences. In recent years, therefore, Adventists have become more and more inoculated against date setting. Those speakers and writers who boldly attempt to set dates, as so many Adventists did in the past, are quickly laughed off by most Adventist audiences. This has led to the tactic of "soft" date setting, much like Andrews did more than a hundred years ago.[73] By "soft" date setting I mean that a person avoids setting a specific time, but instead suggests a general period. They may describe what they are doing as "time study" not "time setting."[74] But if people take statements about a general period seriously, however, setting a decade or a generation is as much date setting as setting a year, a month, or a day.[75]

One author who has focused attention on the year 2000, for example, seeks to avoid the implication of date setting by arguing that the six-thousandth year of earth's history acts not as a specific date for the Second Coming, but as a *terminus ad quem*, a deadline which can be hastened by the actions of God's people.[76] The problem with that position is that the year 2000 is now upon us. The elasticity allowed by the "hastening" is now stretched to its limit. The passage of time will eventually force matters to the ultimate test of authenticity. Fortunately, the author elsewhere does clarify that "There are just enough questions regarding an exact chronology that we cannot determine with precision when the 6000 years will end." He is, nevertheless, confident enough in his time study to have come to believe (by 1994) that "we are the generation that will see the actual, literal, second coming of Christ."[77]

Another way to deflect the charge of date setting is to say, "Here's what I think, but I could be wrong." Persons utilizing this maneuver try to put distance between themselves and their prediction.[78] But here's the problem. If people don't take your prediction seriously, you've just wasted their time presenting it. But if they do take it seriously, you've set a date, no matter what you claim.

Do we need millennial-week theories in order to be convinced that the Lord's coming is near? No, even if the writer or speaker intends otherwise, such schemes only encourage date setting in the minds of others. The millennial-week theory is part of the heritage we have received from the Millerites. Much of that heritage has been a blessing. But we must always subject our heritage to the lessons of Scripture and history. The millennial week is not based on an inspired mandate. F. D. Nichol, long-time editor of the *Review and Herald*, called it "Exhibit A of the fallacy of false analogy."[79] Although writers and speakers may be godly and moderate in their use of the millennial week,[80] history teaches us that timing the final End, even in its "soft" forms, leads to unhealthy excitement. Seventh-day Adventists have rightly discarded the Sunday-keeping and immortality viewpoints of our Millerite heritage. It is time to discard its propensity toward date setting in all its forms, including the use of the millennial week.

> While the [millennial week] theory is intriguing, those who want a clear "Thus saith the Lord" before accepting a teaching will have to admit that such an authority is lacking. Ellen White declares, "Every truth which is essential for us to bring into our practical life, which concerns the salvation of the soul, is made very clear and positive."—*Selected Messages*, book 1, p. 163.[81]

While Ellen White, to my knowledge, never specifically condemns soft date setting,[82] it is interesting that her twelve statements[83] dealing with attempts to date the final events (collected in *Selected Messages*, book 1, pp. 185-192 and *Last Day Events*, pp. 32-36) were all written between 1879 and 1900. All but one were published between 1885 and 1900. This time period fits almost exactly into Andrews's "window of opportunity" for Jesus' return (by the end of the nineteenth century, published in 1883). While Andrews is not the target of any of Ellen White's statements, his articles did provide a broad context in which hard date setters could get a hearing. In my experience, the same thing is happening today.[84]

At the close of the twentieth century it would be well for us to consider the counsel given by Uriah Smith after the close of the previous century.

> There is a long-standing tradition that the week consisting of six days of labor, and the seventh day, or Sabbath of rest, is an emblem of the course of time, spanning the existence of this world in its present condition; that is, that the days represent a thousand years each, the six working days representing six thousand years during which sin and sorrow will reign, and the seventh a thousand years of Sabbatical rest, or the millennium, during which the world will have rest from its trouble, and peace and righteousness will prevail. This, of course, is but conjecture and tradition. But suppose there should be something substantial and tangible to this, it would still be clothed with an element of uncertainty; for the question of chronology, especially in regard to the age of the world, is involved in doubt by the disagreement and confusion of the leading systems of chronology. The question of the nearness of the second coming of Christ is not left to rest upon such a foundation. There are prophecies that indicate approximately the time. Signs bear testimony to the fulfillment of the prophecies; the course of events show the age of the world in which we are living; the apostle says of the church that they are not in darkness that the great day should overtake them as a thief; that is, evidences enough are placed around them that they need not be overtaken as by a thief; and they are told, when they see certain phenomena occurring, to *know* that Christ has reached the very door that opens into the fulfillment of His promises, and the fruition of the hopes of His people.[85]

While Uriah Smith eloquently cautions against all forms of date setting in the above lines, at the same time he certainly does not foresee the possibility that nearly a hundred years later we would still be here. This should remind us to be slow to assert that the coming of Jesus absolutely must occur within this generation. Such statements have been made before by reputable people with no intent to set dates. They have been sadly mistaken in spite of their best efforts to understand the mind of God.

It is my fervent hope that things will wind up in the very near future. But Uriah Smith's sensible words and the result of even his mild attempt to sense the "nearness" of the End remind us not to play God. The End will come when God is ready for it, not before. And just when God will be ready "is not for us to know"[86] until the time itself comes.

---

1. A pre-millennialist is a person who believes that the second coming of Jesus will occur *before* the thousand-year period described in Rev. 20. Seventh-day Adventists are far from alone in this conviction, which I believe is held by the majority of evangelical Protestants.

2. Robert M. Johnston, "6,000 Plus 1,000: Are We Relying on Ancient Speculations to Set Time for the Advent?" *Adventist Review*, October 29, 1998, p. 55.

3. Kyle lists a total of nine separate dates set by Jehovah's Witnesses between 1874 and 1984. See pp. 93-96.

4. P. Gerard Damsteegt, *Foundations of the Seventh-day Adventist Message and Mission* (Grand Rapids, Mich.: William B. Eerdmans Publishing Co., 1977), pp. 37-38; see note 190 for mention of Miller's acceptance of the 6000-year theory. For more detail, see Leroy Edwin Froom, *The Prophetic Faith of Our Fathers: The Historical Development of Prophetic Interpretation* (Hagerstown, Md.: Review and Herald, 1954), vol. 4, pp. 730-733.

5. Johnston, p. 55.

6. G. W. Holt, *Review and Herald*, March 23, 1852, p. 108, and J. B. Cook, *Review and Herald*, August 19, 1851, pp. 10-11, produced articles on the subject fairly early in Seventh-day Adventist experience.

7. John N. Andrews, "The Great Week of Time: Or the Period of Seven Thousand Years Devoted to the Probation and the Judgment of Mankind," *Review and Herald*, July 17, 1883, pp. 456-457; idem, "The Great Week of Time: The Events of the First and Second Thousand Years," *Review and Herald*, July 24, 1883, pp. 472-473; idem, "The Great Week of Time: Events of the Third and Fourth Thousand Years," *Review and Herald*, July 31, 1883, p. 488; idem, "The Great Week of Time: The Events of the Fifth Thousand Years," *Review and Herald*, August 7, 1883, p. 504; idem, "The Great Week of Time: Events of the Sixth Thousand Years," *Review and Herald*, August 14, 1883, pp. 520-521; and idem, "The Great Week of Time: Events of the Seventh Thousand Years," *Review and Herald*, August 21, 1883, pp. 536-537. Pages given here refer to the page number of the volume; since all these references are consecutive, in following notes, only the page will be given.

8. Andrews, p. 456.

9. Andrews, p. 488. Andrews believed that Jesus was born about 5 B.C., which would make the date of Creation 4120 B.C.

10. Andrews, p. 520.

11. Andrews, p. 521.

12. Andrews, p. 536.

13. Note Uriah Smith's response to a reader's question ("In the Question Chair," under the heading "The 7th Thousand Year"), *Review and Herald,* August 13, 1901, p. 523. I am indebted to Johnston's article, cited above, for alerting me to this reference. On the other hand, Dr. O. C. Godsmark, *Youth's Instructor,* September 19, 1901, p. 290 held out for 1902. Smith himself seems to have believed that the six thousand years ended in 1897. Note his hundred-year adjustment of Ussher's chronology in a response to a different question under the heading of "A Question of Chronology. 1 Kings 6:1," *Review and Herald,* March 15, 1892, p. 168.

14. To my knowledge no article supportive of the millennial week has been published in official church journals since 1901. At least four articles have weighed in negatively: Question Corner item "The Six Thousand Years," (unsigned but presumably by editor M. C. Wilcox), *Signs of the Times,* June 7, 1905, p. 6; Question Corner item "World's Age," (again presumably by Wilcox), *Signs of the Times,* September 8, 1909, p. 562; Donald F. Neufeld, "Is the 6,000 Year Theory Valid?" *Review and Herald,* March 25, 1976, p. 10; George W. Reid, "The 6,000-Year Theory Revisited," Windows on the Word, *Adventist Review,* September 27, 1984, p. 9. In addition, F. D. Nichol offered a vigorous critique in *The Midnight Cry* (Hagerstown, Md.: Review and Herald Publishing Association, 1944), pp. 508, 509. On the other side of the scale, a brief positive reference to the "great week of time" concept survived the revision process for the fourth edition of J. N. Andrews and L. R. Conradi's book, *History of the Sabbath and First Day of the Week* (Hagerstown, Md.: Review and Herald Publishing Association, 1912), p. 17. A paragraph-long reference to the millennial week was added to the 1914 edition of *Bible Reading for the Home Circle* (Nampa, Idaho: Pacific Press® Publishing Association, 1914), p. 359. In addition, a chart entitled "The Millennium" was modified in the 1914 edition of *Bible Readings,* p. 356) to make reference to the millennial week (cf. *Bible Readings for the Home Circle,* [Hagerstown, Md.: Review and Herald Publishing Company, 1888], p. 150. The revised chart is reproduced in two other books: W. A. Spicer, *Our Day in the Light of Prophecy* (Nampa, Idaho: Pacfic Press® Publishing Association, 1917), p. 350 and Carlyle B. Haynes, *The return of Jesus* (Hagerstown, Md.: Review and Herald Publishing Association, 1926), p. 294. I am indebted to G. Edward Reid and Warren Johns for most of the above references. My take on all this evidence is that the millennial week survived throughout the century in segments of the popular consciousness, including some in positions of leadership, particularly early in the century. It was always, however, rejected by leadership when it was tied to an attempt to time the coming of Jesus.

15. Johnston, p. 54. The earliest reference seems to be *Jubilees* 4:30. Froom reckoned 2 *Enoch* 33:1, 2 ("the first seven [days of Creation] revolve in the form of the seven thousand, and that at the beginning of the eighth thousand there should be a time of

not-counting, endless. . . .") to be another pre-Christian witness to Jewish belief in the millennial week. See LeRoy Edwin Froom, *The Prophetic Faith of Our Fathers*, 1, pp. 195, 196. But the earliest manuscript dates to the fourteenth century, and there is now grave doubt that the work existed before the Middle Ages. See James Hamilton Charlesworth, editor, *The Old Testament Pseudepigrapha* (Garden City, N.Y.: Doubleday, 1983), vol. 1, pp. 94, 95; see also Charlesworth, *The Old Testament Pseudepigrapha and the New Testament: Prolegomena for the Study of Christian Origins* (Cambridge: Cambridge University Press, 1985), pp. 32-35.

16. Johnston, p. 55. The best known expression of the millennial week can be found in the tractate *Sanhedrin* 97a and b. There reference is made to Rabbi Kattina who said, "Six thousand years shall the world exist, and one it shall be desolate."

17. Ibid., p. 55.

18. *Epistle of Barnabas* 13:4-9.

19. For a detailed exposition of the views of Barnabas, Hippolytus, and other early Church Fathers on the age of the earth, see Richard Landes, "Lest the Millennium Be Fulfilled: Apocalyptic Expectations and the Pattern of Western Chronography 100-800 CE," in *The Use and Abuse of Eschatology in the Middle Ages*, edited by Werner Verbeke, Daniel Verhelst, and Andries Welkenhuysen (Louvain: Leuven University Press, 1988), pp.141-165.

20. Landes, pp. 138-141. See also the discussion in the previous chapter on the year 1000.

21. Ussher was far from alone at that time in his interest in chronology. See Froom, vol. 2, p. 430.

22. Johnston, p. 55.

23. G. Edward Reid, *Even at the Door* (by the author, printed by Review and Herald Graphics, Hagerstown, Md., 1994). Note particularly his reference to both the "6000-year theory" and the year 2000 on p. 203. In personal correspondence, however, he has assured me that it was not his intention to focus anyone's attention on the year 2000. While he continues to believe that the Bible and the Spirit of Prophecy support the millennial week concept, he wishes to argue only that we are near the end of the 6000 years. He affirms: "I have never attempted to work out a chronology and do not plan to do so." G. Edward Reid, email message to Jon Paulien on January 19, 1999.

24. Ibid., p. 10.

25. Ibid., pp. 10-11.

26. Ibid., pp. 23, 85-87, 90-93.

27. Ibid., pp. 87-89.

28. Ibid., pp. 95-97. Reid quotes Dan. 8:15-19 and places it in association with Ellen White's statement, "There is a day that God hath appointed for the close of this world's history," (*Special Testimonies on Education*, p. 107).

29. Reid, pp. 107-108.

30. Ibid., pp. 108-119.

31. Ibid., p. 126.

32. Reid argues the connection between the millennium and the Babylonian captivity

(Jer. 4:23-27) which 2 Chron. 36:20-21 connects to the Sabbath cycle of Lev. 25:1-7 (I would add Lev. 26:33-35 to the mix). Thus, for Reid, the millennium becomes the Sabbath of the millennial week. See pp. 117, 128.

33. Ellen White, *The Great Controversy*, p. 656.

34. Donald F. Neufeld, "Footnote to the 6,000-Year Theory," *Review and Herald*, May 13, 1976, p. 10.

35. Such as that found in the *Talmud* and the *Epistle of Barnabas*.

36. See, for example, the work of Edwin Richard Thiele in *The Mysterious Numbers of the Hebrew Kings*, third edition (Grand Rapids, Mich: Zondervan, 1983).

37. The Dead Sea Scrolls make it clear that there were at least three major Hebrew text traditions in existence in the time of Jesus. The "Babylonian" or "proto-Masoretic" text tradition was the precursor of the Hebrew text of our Bibles today, the "proto-Samaritan" or "ancient Palestinian" text which is the precursor of the Samaritan Pentateuch of today, and the "Egyptian" Hebrew text that lies behind the Greek translation called the Septuagint. See Geza Vermes, *The Dead Sea Scrolls: Qumran in Perspective* (Philadelphia: Fortress Press, 1977), p. 206; and James C. VanderKam, *The Dead Sea Scrolls Today* (Grand Rapids, Mich.: William B. Eerdmans, 1994), pp. 123-126. For a more comprehensive overview of what is known about the Old Testament text see Emmanuel Tov, "Textual Criticism (Old Testament)," *The Anchor Bible Dictionary*, edited by David Noel Freedman (New York: Doubleday, 1992), vol. 6, pp. 393-412. The Septuagint text provides the longest chronology of the Old Testament period and the Samaritan the shortest.

38. Landes, "Use and Abuse," pp. 138, 144-149.

39. Schwartz, pp. 24-26. Reid argues for the superiority of the Masoretic text as a basis for Biblical chronology (p. 155). While most Old Testament scholars would agree in principle, the Masoretic text does not seem to be the basis for the Bible used by most New Testament writers and early Christians. My purpose here is simply to show that the Bible cannot be used to establish the millennial week with any certainty.

40. Saul Leeman, "Was Bishop Ussher's Chronology Influenced by a Midrash?" *Semeia* 8 (1977): 127-130; James Barr, "Why the World Was Created in 4004 B.C.: Archbishop Ussher and Biblical Chronology," *Bulletin of the John Rylands University Library of Manchester* 67 (Spring, 1985): 578-590.

41. For a more detailed examination of these issues see the chapter entitled "A Recent Creation," in Randy Younker, *God's Creation* (Nampa, Idaho: Pacific Press, 1999).

42. See also Paul's use of the same phrase in 1 Thess. 5:1-3.

43. *Selected Messages*, book 1, p. 188.

44. Our examination of this text is necessarily brief. The reader is referred to Richard J. Bauckham, *Jude, 2 Peter*, Word Biblical Commentary, 50 (Waco, Tx.: Word Books, 1983), pp. 306-310, for a thorough examination of this text and its relationship to millennial week theories.

45. Ibid, pp. 296, 307.

46. James Moffat, *The General Epistles James, Peter, and Judas*, The Moffat New Testament Commentary (London: Hodder and Stoughton, 1928), p. 207.

47. Zdravko Stefanovic points out that in oriental culture (the culture of the Bible) the importance of a person was and is measured by the delay of their arrival. The more important the person, the longer the delay ("Delay? What Delay? Seeing the Impending Advent Through Oriental Eyes," *Adventist Review*, October 29, 1998, pp. 69-70).

48. Bauckham, p. 309.

49. James H. Charlesworth, *The Old Testament Pseudepigrapha*, vol. 1, Apocalyptic Literature and Testaments (Garden City, N.Y.: Doubleday, 1983), p. 636.

50. While Peter clearly refers to hastening the coming in 2 Pet. 3:11 (endorsed by E. G. White in *Desire of Ages*, p. 633, and *Testimonies for the Church*, vol. 8, pp. 22-23), Ellen White is explicit regarding the human role in delaying the coming as well (see *Evangelism*, pp. 695-696).

51. Reid, pp. 107, 157-158.

52. Ibid., p. 11.

53. Ibid., pp. 135-136.

54. With reference to the beginning of the millennium she says: "For six thousand years, Satan's work of rebellion has 'made the earth to tremble'." *The Great Controversy*, p. 659.

55. For example, *Signs of the Times*, May 8, 1884, p. 273; *The Great Controversy*, p. 518; *Patriarchs and Prophets*, p. 342.

56. *Review and Herald*, July 28, 1874, p. 51; *The Great Controversy*, p. 548; *Desire of Ages*, p. 48.

57. Warren H. Johns, "Ellen G. White and the Age of the Earth," unpublished paper by the author, final draft May, 1995.

58. *Spirit of Prophecy*, vol. 1, p. 87; *Signs of the Times*, May 8, 1884, p. 273.

59. *Spiritual Gifts*, vol. 3, p. 92; *The Great Controversy*, p. x (Introduction).

60. *The Story of Jesus*, p. 183; *Signs of the Times*, September 29, 1887, p. 593.

61. Johns, p. 9.

62. Johns, pp. 13-15; cf. Johnston, p. 55.

63. *Spiritual Gifts*, vol. 3, pp. 229-230; *Patriarchs and Prophets*, p. 267; *Signs of the Times*, August 24, 1891, p. 269. These statements indicate 400-430 years from the call of Abraham to the Exodus. Since Isaac appears to have lived his entire 186 years in Palestine, the period of slavery in Egypt would be around 200 years.

64. *Review and Herald*, January 9, 1894, p. 17; *Desire of Ages*, p. 32; *Testimonies*, 8, p. 207. In these statements the period of *slavery* is 400 years. See Johns, p. 4.

65. William H. Shea, "Ellen White on the Length of the Sojourn," unpublished paper by the author. Pages 12-27 are titled, "Ellen G. White and the 6000 Years" and speak directly to the issue of this chapter.

66. Ibid., p. 2.

67. Taking the Hebrew Old Testament in a straightforward manner and correlating with the best extrabiblical evidence (comets, eclipses and historical records) one comes to about 4110 years from Creation to the birth of Christ. There are 1656 years from Creation to the Flood (Gen. 5), 367 years from the Flood to the call of Abraham (Gen. 11), 215 from the call to Jacob's transfer to Egypt (25 years to the birth of Isaac [Gen.

12:4; 21:5], 60 years to the birth of Jacob [Gen. 25:26] who was 130 when he went to Egypt [Gen. 47:9]), 430 years in Egypt (Exod. 12:40-41), 480 years from the Exodus to the construction of the temple (1 Kings 6:1), which was about 962 years before the birth of Christ. This is very close to Andrews' conclusion and would put the end of the 6000 years around 1885, the exact spot at which Johns feels Ellen White moves to a "more than 6000 years" stance. It is possible, of course, to play with the ambiguities between these texts and others in the Old and New Testaments.

68. Shea, pp. 24-25. In fact, Shea points out, her very last statement in 1913 contains the adjective "nearly." Johns responds that it is likely that Ellen White's assistants added the word "nearly" to an earlier statement (see Johns, p. 9, note 1). I am not sure who is right on this point.

69. *Selected Messages*, book 1, p. 188.

70. Ibid., book 1, p. 189.

71. *Last Day Events*, pp. 35-36.

72. *Review and Herald*, August 2, 1881, p. 89.

73. Instead of "soft date-setting" Kyle uses the phrase "implicit date-setting," Kyle, p. 199. Not only Andrews, but also James White took a shot at soft date-setting when he argued that the generation that saw the falling of the stars and proclaimed the Millerite message related to 1844 would witness the scenes connected with the coming of Jesus. See James White, *Life Incidents*, 1 (Battle Creek: Steam Press of the Seventh-day Adventist Publishing Association, 1868), pp. 338-340. Note his denunciation of hard date-setting on page 322 of the same book!

74. Some may recognize in this sentence the language of Larry Wilson, another popular writer and speaker who saw a lot of potential significance in the dates around 1994, on the basis of Jubilee calculations. Wilson assures me that he never intended to suggest a "hard" date for Jesus' return or any of the events that would precede His return. He understood the 1994 date as ushering in the final end-time period, but without specifying how long that would be. Since he sees no particular significance in the year 2000 I have chosen not to examine his views in detail here, but I hope to do so at a future time.

75. Gorden R. Doss, "Ready for His Appearing," *Adventist Review*, October 29, 1998, p. 61.

76. Reid, pp. 136-137. This interpretation of Reid's intention is confirmed by his comment in a more recent interview article: "My personal judgment is He *could* come early, but He will *not* come late—not beyond 6,000 years (emphasis Reid's)." Andy Nash, "Ed Reid: Proclaiming the End," *Adventist Review*, February 18, 1999, p. 15.

77. Reid, p. 10. Some of the consequences of date setting in all its forms are detailed in *What the Bible Says About the End-Time*, pp. 20-27, and 152-154.

78. Doss, p. 61.

79. F. D. Nichol, *The Midnight Cry* (Hagerstown, Md.: Review and Herald Publishing Association, 1944), p. 508.

80. J. N. Andrews and G. Edward Reid are examples of such a moderate use.

81. Neufeld, "Is the 6,000-Year Theory Valid?" p. 11.

82. She even appears to practice it on three or four occasions. See *Early Writings*, p. 58; *Testimonies*, vol. 1, pp. 131, 132; *Review and Herald*, July 31, 1888, p. 482; *Review and Herald*, December 27, 1898, p. 825. But what a prophet is led to do in a specific circumstance by direct leading of God (offer a conditional prophecy) is often inappropriate for those of us who lack a similar divine mandate.

83. Of the fifteen statements listed in *Selected Messages*, book 1 and *Last Day Events*, three are duplications. *Testimonies for the Church*, vol. 4, p. 307 (1879) is quoted twice in *Last Day Events* (pp. 33 and 34); *Review and Herald*, March 22, 1892, pp. 177-178 is quoted in *Selected Messages*, book 1, pp. 185-191 and *Last Day Events*, p. 33; and Letter 28, 1897 (quoted in *Last Day Events*, p. 33) is also the source of *Selected Messages*, book 2, p. 84 (quoted in *Last Day Events*, p. 35).

84. I don't want to make too much of this insight without further study. For one thing, the compilations may have been incomplete. In a sermon delivered in 1891 and published in 1892, Ellen White remembers addressing the issue of time setting as early as 1851 (*Selected Messages*, book 1, pp. 188-189). My point is, the last word on Ellen White's view of this subject has probably not been written yet, so it is unwise to base the millennial-week theory on the evidence currently known.

85. Uriah Smith, "The 7th Thousand Year," *Review and Herald*, August 13, 1901, p. 523.

86. Acts 1:7.

CHAPTER 6

A.D. 2001: Then What?

Richard Landes, historian and director of Boston University's Center for Millennial Studies, expects that the arrival of the year 2001 will bring about a devastating "millennial disappointment." Alarmists of all stripes, Christian and non-Christian, are expected to be "totally discredited."[1] If "The End Of The World As We Know It" turns out to be a non-event, many Seventh-day Adventists may find themselves in a personal crisis of faith. It is, above all, for them that this chapter was written.

I fervently hope that those who see special significance in the year 2000 are right, even if for the wrong reason. The coming of our Lord is really the only hope for the human race. But what if we reach the year 2001 and nothing unusual happens? What then? If time should last a while longer, how shall we then live? How can we maintain that balance between a fervent expectation of the nearness of Jesus' return with a sober and patient willingness to occupy and plan until the day He comes? In this chapter I will attempt to lay out some basic principles designed to help us keep our balance in exciting times.

4—M.B.

PRINCIPLE 1: BALANCE EXPECTATION AND ENDURANCE

How can Adventists maintain a balance between eager expectation of the soon coming of Jesus and a sober, steady endurance that plans for the long haul? This balance is hard to achieve and easy to lose. And it affects many day-to-day decisions. For example, an out-of-balance conviction that the Lord is coming soon can lead to unfortunate consequences.

Here at Andrews University, for example, we are in the process of replacing two buildings. Griggs Hall was completed in the early 1940s, yet it is no longer a suitable venue for classrooms and faculty offices. Seminary Hall was built in the early 1960s, yet it is badly in need of renovation. At the University of Chicago, on the other hand, most buildings were built in the nineteenth century, yet they remain serviceable and attractive, so age should not be a problem. But when Adventists build, we are tempted to build for the short haul. "Why not save a little here and there, after all the Lord is coming soon."

Let me give a specific illustration. When the Seminary was built, presumably in order to save money, only the shady (north) side of the building was air-conditioned. That means that the faculty can stay cool in summer whenever they are not in class. But classes (where the learning for which the building was built is supposed to take place) are taught in the sunny (south) half of the building. That means summer classes melt in the warmth and humidity of Michigan summers. At times it is nearly impossible to go on. The result of such decisions is that it will take around ten million dollars to replace Griggs Hall and to renovate and expand Seminary Hall. How much better it would have been if our pioneers had planned for the long haul!

A related area is endowments. To this day many Adventists criticize the drive to build educational endowments as a lack of faith in the soon return of Jesus. The reality is that the lack of endowments has placed Adventist colleges and universities at a huge financial disadvantage in comparison with most other private schools. The Lord desires us to anticipate His return, but not at the expense of preparing for the possibility that our children and grandchildren may have to live with our decisions.

When I decided to leave the pastorate and begin doctoral studies, a church official argued against it saying, "You'll just be wasting your time.

The Lord will come before you finish." I was inclined to agree with him at the time, but how glad I am today (twenty years later) that I chose to ignore his advice.

On the other hand we do not want to fall into the trap of the wicked servant who says, "My Master is staying away a long time" (Matt. 24:48). The continual passage of spectacular events, and the failure of many foolish predictions can lead one to question whether the End will ever come. We can become absorbed with this life to the neglect of preparation for the age to come. But we must not forget that "Christians have always anticipated the imminent return of Christ. When we lose our sense of urgency, we lose part of our message."[2]

If we cannot be certain that Jesus is coming in this decade or this generation, however, in what sense can we really use the term "soon"? Haven't Christians spoken of the Second Coming as soon for almost 2000 years? In what sense can anyone call themselves "Adventist" (those looking forward to the soon return of Jesus) anymore?

We should keep in mind that the same chapter in which Jesus says that no one knows the day or the hour (Matt 24:36) also offers indications as to when the coming is near (Matt 24:33). Adventists tend to evaluate "nearness" from a Western chronological perspective. But what is "near" in terms of time? A day? A year? A decade? A century? The author of Revelation considered Jesus' coming to be near by A.D. 95 (Rev 1:3; 22:10,12). So a chronological understanding of "nearness" is clearly false in light of the passage of 2000 years since the New Testament was written. But from an Eastern perspective nearness is much more a state of mind than a chronological datum. We need to find a way of saying that the coming of Jesus is near without insisting that it has to be in this decade or this generation.

But is there any sense that the coming of Jesus is chronologically nearer now than it was in the first century? Note Ellen White's comment on the evidence in Matt 24:33, 36, "One saying of the Saviour must not be made to destroy another. Though no man knoweth the *day* nor the *hour* of His coming, we are instructed and required to know when it is near (emphasis hers)."[3] For Ellen White the coming *was* near because the time prophecies leading to the time of the End had been fulfilled.

Bible prophecy marks out the path we follow from the Cross to the Second Coming. With the passing of the great time prophecies of Daniel and Revelation we are now living in the time of the End. So these are not just ordinary times. The year 2000 is much closer to the End than the year 1000 was. We know that since 1798 and 1844 this world's history is writing its final chapter. While we cannot know with certainty that this is the final generation, we certainly know that things can wind up very soon. Having said that, however, what happened in 1844 gives us no direct information as to whether we are living in the last decade or even the last generation. We need to be prepared as if it is and prepared if it is not.

We can take further encouragement from the events outlined in the early chapters of this book. While current events should not be used to encourage date setting in any of its forms, hard or soft, we are certainly living in times like those the Bible associates with the End. Knowledge is increasing with breathtaking rapidity (Dan. 12:4). The Internet and satellite broadcasting make it possible for the whole world to hear the gospel in a short time (Matt. 24:14). The growth of the Seventh-day Adventist Church in some areas of the world is a token of the final movements, which will be rapid ones. Divisions among nations are increasing. Weapons of mass destruction are in increasingly unstable hands. Rebellion, profanity, perversions, and violence are increasing (2 Tim. 3:1-5). The Bible says, "When these things begin to happen, get up, lift up your heads, for your redemption is drawing near" (Luke 21:28, my translation).

Let me remind you of the beautiful balance in a statement quoted earlier in this book.

> You will not be able to say that He will come in one, two, or five years, neither are you to put off His coming by stating that it may not be for ten or twenty years (*Selected Messages*, book 1, p. 189).

We certainly don't know when Jesus will come. But we must not make the mistake of thinking that the End, therefore, must be far away. True "Adventists" live life with a sense of tension between occupying until He comes and anticipating that He will come soon. We want the Lord to come, we believe He's coming soon, yet we need to fill each day with the responsibilities that God has given to us. How do we keep that biblical tension healthy in our personal and corporate experience? The following principles are intended to be helpful.

PRINCIPLE 2: WE DON'T NEED TO KNOW WHEN

God has created human beings with a natural tendency toward curiosity. And one of the things we are most curious about is the future. Going beyond the clear teachings of the Bible about the future doesn't automatically make someone a bad person. He or she is simply being human, exercising natural human curiosity. In fact, curiosity is the basic driving force behind all successful research. But when we try to determine the timing of the Second Coming or of earth's final events we are being curious about matters that belong only to God (Acts 1:6-7; Matt. 24:36). "The secret things belong to the Lord our God" (Deut. 29:29).

Over and over again Ellen White was forced to confront situations in which people sought to make the timing of the End an issue. She was consistent in her support of the biblical counsel:

> I plainly stated at the Jackson camp meeting to these fanatical parties that they were doing the work of the adversary of souls; they were in darkness. They claimed to have great light that probation would close in October, 1884. I there stated in public that the Lord had been pleased to show me that there would be no definite time in the message given of God since 1844 (*Last Day Events*, pp. 35-36).

> There will always be false and fanatical movements made by persons in the church who claim to be led of God—those who will run before they are sent and will give day and date for the occurrence of unfulfilled prophecy. The enemy is pleased to have them do this, for their successive failures and leading into false lines cause confusion and unbelief (*Selected Messages*, book 2, p.84).

Paul underlines this limitation to our curiosity in 1 Thess. 5. Evidently, people in the Thessalonian church were saying, "Paul, when is

Jesus going to come?" But he indicates that this is a question that cannot be answered:

> Now, brothers,
>> about times and dates
>> we do not need to write to you,
>> for you know very well
>> that the day of the Lord will come
>> like a thief in the night.
>>> 1 Thess. 5:1, 2

Paul warns the Thessalonians not to be obsessed with the timing of Jesus' coming, His coming will be like a thief, the exact timing will be a total surprise. How did Paul know that? Because Jesus had said it already (see Matt 24:43, 44). Can any of you predict when a thief will come to your house? Of course not. The Second Coming is not an event that human beings will be able to time in advance. But here Paul makes a crucial point.

> But you, brothers,
>> are not in darkness
>> so that this day should surprise you
>> like a thief.
> You are all sons of the light
>> and sons of the day.
>> We do not belong to the night
>> or to the darkness.
>>> 1 Thess. 5:4, 5

Paul says that although the time of Jesus' coming is a surprise, His people won't be surprised because they will be ready for it. You don't know when the thief will come but you can be ready. All setting of dates is at best an approximation, at worst a spiritual nightmare. But the good news is that you don't need to know just when Jesus is going to come to be ready for His coming. The goal is to be ready now, to be always ready.

More on this in the last chapter of this book.

If "knowing the when" is not the task of Christians waiting for End, what should we be doing with our time while we wait? In 1 Thess. 5:12-24 Paul offers a series of suggestions for Christian attention as we approach the End. "Adventists" should have a high regard for leadership (1 Thess. 5:12-13) and live in peace with each other (5:13). We should be encouraging, patient, kind, joyful and thankful (5:14-18). We need to pray continually (17), let the Spirit work (19), hold prophecy in high regard (20), test everything (21) and avoid all kinds of evil (22). And as focus on the Second Coming increases, we are to allow God to sanctify us through and through so that we will be found blameless at the coming of our Lord Jesus Christ (23-24). Sounds pretty busy to me. No wonder the Bible does not allot any time for figuring out when Jesus is going to come!

PRINCIPLE 3: THE END IS ABOUT JESUS

One problem with a focus on the timing of the End is that it distracts from the biblical perspective on End-time events; above all else the End is about Jesus. In Christian understanding whenever the Old Testament points toward the future, Jesus is at the center of it all. He is the offspring (NIV: or seed) of the woman in Gen. 3:15, who will one day crush the serpent's head. He is the offspring (or seed) of Abraham in Gen. 22:18, through whom all nations on earth will be blessed. He is the star that will come out of Jacob, according to Num. 24:15-19, who will destroy the enemies of Israel. He is the prophet like Moses (Deut. 18:15-19) who will speak the words of the Lord. He is the king like David (Isa. 11:11-16; Jer. 23:5-6) who will fear the Lord, reign wisely, uplift the poor, and do the right thing. He is the king who will ride into Jerusalem on a donkey and proclaim peace to the nations who submit to his rule (Zech. 9:9-10; Mic. 4:8). He is the son of man who receives dominion over the earth like that of the first Adam (Dan. 7:13-14).

The above list only scratches the surface. A careful reading of chapters three and four in my book *What the Bible Says About the End-Time* goes into more depth on a few of the above concepts. But there is much more to this theme in the Old Testament than simply lies on the surface. The New Testament portrays Jesus as the fulfillment of all Old Testament history and experience. Jesus is the second Adam (Rom. 5:12-21: 1 Cor. 15:40-49), the new Isaac (Matt. 1:1; Heb. 11:17-19), the new Moses (Acts 3:22-24), the future of Israel (Hos. 11:1; Matt. 2:14-15), the new David (Matt. 1:1; 22:41-46), the new Solomon (Matt. 12:42), and the new Cyrus (Rev. 16:12; cf. Isa. 44:26-28; 45:1-14).

For the writers of the New Testament, therefore, Jesus is what the End is all about. In His earthly ministry, the Kingdom has come (Matt. 12:28), in His death and resurrection the judgment of the End has come (John 12:31; Rom. 8:3), through His heavenly ministry his followers experience heaven now (Eph. 2:7), at His second coming the End will have truly come (1 Cor. 15:20-28). It is because of Christ that God fulfills all the End-time promises to Israel:

> For no matter how many promises God has made,
>   they are "Yes" in Christ.
>   And so through Him the "Amen" is spoken by us
>   to the glory of God.
>   2 Cor. 1:20

God's promises are fulfilled to those who meet the conditions. But according to 2 Cor. 1:20, the conditions to all God's promises, even the End-time ones, have been met through the actions of Christ. Jesus is the faithful Israelite who has fully obeyed Israel's covenant with God and has therefore reaped all the blessings and promises of that covenant. The New Testament views all things in terms of Christ; He is ultimately all that matters.

A view of the End that centers in Christ rather than in current events guards the interpreter against the excesses of speculation. If one's view of the End focuses on having more and more of Christ one is not so driven to calculate just when He will come. Although Jesus' return seems delayed, we know that it was *Jesus* who promised to return. We can trust *His* promise.

PRINCIPLE 4: FALLING IN LOVE WITH JESUS

The answer to the problem of lackluster and disinterested Christians, therefore, is not to continuously trumpet the immediacy of the End, or to major in the sins and shortcomings of other Adventists. The New Testament offers an entirely different approach to developing and maintaining a fervent expectation of Jesus' return. It was the conviction of the New Testament writers that, with the coming of the Messiah, a taste of the life of heaven arrived for all who believe in Jesus. This is no fiction. Those in Christ get a real taste, a "down payment" on the heavenly inheritance, while still living in the real world (Eph. 1:13, 14).

Those who taste the heavenly experience now by faith will never lose their anticipation of Jesus' return. When you taste Him and the powers of the coming age every day, your desire for more of Him will be constant no matter how long the Second Coming may seem delayed. But if your longing for His return is tied to a date, the longing can only last so long; when the date passes, the longing usually passes with it. New Testament anticipation of the Second Coming is grounded not on the timing of the End, but on the experience of eternal life with Christ as a present reality by faith. Those who have tasted the joys of heaven now will anticipate even greater joys at His return. Those who are living in the experience of the "kingdom" *now* by faith, will be ready when the ultimate kingdom comes.

Within Adventist thinking there seems to be a serious lack of emphasis on the New Testament teaching that the reality of Jesus' eternal kingdom is already here (Matt. 11:2-15; 12:28; Luke 4:18-21; John 5:24-25). When the Pharisees asked Jesus about the future kingdom He directed their attention away from the future to the present (Luke 17:21). If the reality of the kingdom is already here, our attention will focus not so much on the future as on the events of the kingdom that are already present in Christ. This is what keeps expectation fresh; a living and daily experience of the kingdom! Ellen White seems to have expressed the implication of the above in the following statement:

The shortness of time is urged as an incentive for us to seek righteousness and to make Christ our friend. This is not the great motive. It savors of selfishness. Is it necessary that the terrors of the day of God be held before us to compel us through fear to right action? This ought not to be. *Jesus is attractive* (*Review and Herald*, August 2, 1881, p. 89, emphasis mine).

Many sincere Christians believe that continually calling attention to the shortness of the time is the key to encouraging readiness for the End. The above statement by Ellen White exposes the dark underbelly of what may seem pious on the surface. To encourage readiness on the basis of the shortness of time is to appeal to fear and selfishness. Motives such as these pale in significance when compared with the surpassing attractiveness of Jesus.

Overplaying the shortness of the End is a poor substitute for the kind of relationship with Jesus that the New Testament proclaims. If you feel a constant need for the excitement of date setting and speculations regarding current events, I point you instead to Jesus, who can fill the emptiness without the side effects! If you are weighed down with the cares of this life, and have lost your taste for Christ's return, I invite you to renew your relationship with Him. Those who are in love with Jesus will be ready to meet Him when He comes.

PRINCIPLE 5: ATTACK COMPLACENCY

Since the Bible, rightly understood, contains true information about the End, it is as hazardous to ignore its teachings about the End as it is to distort them the way the time-setters and the speculators do. The best way to attack End-time complacency is a wholehearted openness to the Word of God wherever it may lead. The excitement of Bible discovery that leads to ever-increasing relationship with Jesus is a marvelous antidote to spiritual lethargy. But how can we safeguard our study of the Bible from the kinds of speculative excesses that seem so common among those who long for Jesus' return? I'd like to suggest five approaches to Bible study that can keep us in the solid center of the biblical message.

1. Study in the context of much prayer and an attitude of self-distrust. Our hearts are naturally deceitful (Jer. 17:9). By nature we lack a teachable spirit. It doesn't matter how much Greek you know or how many Ph.D.s you accumulate, if you don't have a teachable spirit, your learning is worth nothing. True knowledge of God does not come from merely intellectual pursuit or academic study (John 7:16,17; 1 Cor. 2:14; James 1:5).

According to 2 Thess. 2:10, the knowledge of God comes from a willingness to receive the truth from God no matter what it costs. The gifts of God are free, but they can be costly in their own way. Knowledge of God can cost your life, family, friends, and reputation. But if you are willing to find the truth no matter what the cost, you will receive it.

Bible study needs to begin with what I call authentic prayer. The prayer I'm suggesting might go something like this: "Lord, I want the truth no matter what the cost to me personally." That's a hard prayer to pray. But if you pray that prayer, you will receive God's truth. And you will also pay the price. Furthermore, as we have seen, the truth about the End is the truth about Jesus. We will want to know Jesus no matter what the cost. And He is eager to respond and show Himself to us.

2. **Use a variety of translations.** It is imperative that those who have no access to the Greek and Hebrew of the Bible consult a variety of translations of a biblical text when doing serious study of the Bible. Every translation has its limitations and weaknesses and to some degree reflects the biases of the translator(s). These limitations can be minimized by comparing several translations against each other. Where most translators agree, the underlying Greek text is probably fairly plain and can be safely followed. When there is wide disagreement among the translators, the original is probably difficult or ambiguous. A translation that deviates widely from all others generally signals the translator's biases.

Where translation patterns indicate that the original text is clear, we can safely base our authority on the translated text. Where the translation patterns indicate that a text we are seeking to understand is ambiguous or difficult to translate, it would not be safe to base our teaching and practice on a particular translation of that text.

3. **Spend the majority of your time in the clear texts of Scripture.** If you want to really let the Scriptures speak for themselves, spend the majority of your time in the sections of Scripture that are reasonably clear. There are many parts of the Bible regarding which there is little disagreement among Christians, while other texts vex even the Greek and Hebrew scholars. So an extremely important safeguard in the study of Scripture is to spend the majority of your time in the sections that are reasonably clear. The clear texts of Scripture ground the reader in the great central themes of the biblical message, safeguarding the interpreter against

the misuse of texts that are more ambiguous.

On the other hand, if you spend the majority of your time in texts like the seals and trumpets of Revelation or Daniel 11, you *will* go crazy. One of the major tactics of people who misuse the Bible is to take ambiguous texts, develop creative solutions to the problems they find there, and then use those solutions as the basis for their theology. Such interpreters often end up having to distort clear texts of Scripture because the message there doesn't fit the theology that they have developed from the difficult texts.

As a case in point, scholarship on 2 Peter 3 demonstrates that the author's "one day is like a thousand years" statement is not one of the clearest texts in the Bible.[4] Seeing the millennial week concept in 2 Pet. 3:8 is, at best, one possible reading of the text. To make a difficult text like 2 Pet. 3:8 the cornerstone of a major theory will likely lead an interpreter to underplay some of the clearer texts in the Bible, thus short-circuiting inspiration.

4. **Spend the majority of your study time reading the Bible** rather than searching a concordance. An obsession with detail can lead you away from the central thrust of the Bible. Our study of the millennial-week theory shows that you can put Bible texts together in such a way as to prove almost anything you want to prove. Without safeguards concordance study tends to focus on texts apart from their contexts.

Concordance study is all the more dangerous when it is done on a computer. Thanks to the computer it is possible to spend hundreds of hours in "Bible study" without ever actually reading the Bible itself. The meanings you can draw from such study may be extremely impressive, yet have nothing to do with the original writer's intention. It can be like taking a pair of scissors and cutting fifty texts out of your Bible, tossing them like a salad in a bowl, and finally pulling them out one by one and saying, "This is from the Lord." Whether the concordance is a print version or is computerized, the process results in putting the interpreter in control of how the biblical text impacts on his or her understanding of truth.

When you read biblical books from beginning to end, on the other hand, the biblical author is in control of the order and flow of the material. The author leads you naturally from one idea to the next, your exposure to the Bible is not controlled by any need arising from within yourself or from your background. Broad reading of the Bible, therefore, anchors the interpreter in the intentions of the original writers and helps the interpreter to get the "big picture" view that provides the best safeguard against bizarre interpretations of its isolated parts. General reading naturally encourages a teachable spirit and helps you see the text as it was intended to be read. The Bible is not supposed to learn from us; we are supposed to learn from the Bible.

With regard to the topic of this book, the millennial-week theory cannot be built on a reading approach to the Scriptures. It is clearly not an intentional teaching of any Bible writer. Instead the theory must be built by analogy upon a comparison of texts whose relationship is not always self-evident. While such an approach to texts can help us expand our theological understanding of the Bible, it is safest when built upon the clear statements and intentions of the biblical writers.

5. Give careful attention to the criticism of peers (people who give similar attention to the Bible as you do) especially those who disagree with you or who are competent in the original languages and the tools of exegesis. One of the biggest problems in biblical understanding is that each of us has a natural bent to self-deception (Jer. 17:9). That self-deception runs so deep that sometimes, even if you are using the original text, praying, and doing a lot of general reading in the clear texts of the Bible, it is still possible to end up in a completely bizarre place. The best antidote to self-deception is to constantly subject one's own understandings to the criticism of others who are making equally rigorous efforts to understand those texts.

It may be painful to listen to that kind of criticism. Nevertheless, such criticisms are particularly valuable when they come from people we naturally disagree with. People who disagree with us see things in the text that we would never see because of our particular blind spots and defense mechanisms. A sister in the church may be just as unteachable as I am, but if she has a different set of blind spots than I do, she will see things in the text that I would miss and I will see things that she would miss.

No one who studies the Bible with earnest prayer and self-distrust can remain complacent about the End. And those who saturate themselves in the big picture of the Bible that comes from broad reading of the clear texts, corrected by vigorous listening to others, will stay out of the pit of sensationalism and date setting.

PRINCIPLE 6: WATCH EVENTS WITH CARE

Seventh-day Adventists know that we are living in the time of the End. We have become accustomed to watching world events with great interest and comparing them with what we know from Bible prophecy. And it has never been easier to stay informed. With the help of the Internet it is not difficult to amass a huge quantity of information about world affairs in a short period of time. The first two chapters of this book, for example, are based on information that is free and readily available, some of which is far more insightful than the average news magazine. But one needs to make use of such information with great care.

Recently, for example, someone came across an Executive Order from the U.S. President that forbids the hoarding of vital supplies, including food and fuel. "Survivalists" among us saw this as setting the stage for the decree that God's people can neither buy nor sell when the End time comes (Rev. 13:16-17). Excitement began to build until someone pointed out that the decree in question was issued in 1950, in the context of the Korean War crisis. The response then came that the decree was never rescinded and that President Clinton could use it to bring about the final events in short order. No doubt he or his successor could. But a decree made back in 1950 tells us nothing about the likelihood that Jesus will come around the year 2000.

There is a twofold problem when it comes to keeping up with current events in the midst of the Information Age. First, within this enormous mass of information one must distinguish between information which is sound and that which is simply someone's empty speculation forwarded around from computer to computer. Second, even when the information is clearly solid (as is the case with potential date-change problems in computer networks), one still has to soberly evaluate whether that solid information is of any spiritual significance.

It is no easy matter to determine which sources of information are generally sound and which are not. It helps to become familiar with a news source's track record over time, with its biases, and with its reasons for offering information on the Internet. The CIA home page, for example, offers some solid information but only when that information is readily available elsewhere. And there is always the possibility that disinformation is mixed in with truth for national security purposes. An intelligence operation like Stratfor Corporation, on the other hand, is much more forthcoming and reliable (they are trying to sell you on how good they are), but still achieves only about 70% accuracy. After all, even the CIA knows a lot less about world events than it would like. Sites like the Drudge Report and Koenig's Watch are far more speculative (read: gossip) than Stratfor or the CIA, yet there are nuggets of solid data from time to time that may appear nowhere else. Congressional records, on the other hand, have an aura of vanilla-flavored reliability, yet information is sometimes made public or withheld for political purposes.

The bottom line is that current events watching is exciting but accuracy requires a great deal of discernment and experience. The average Christian must be slow to accept the latest report or conspiracy theory, especially when reliable filters like major news organizations or church papers are silent on the subject. I am amazed sometimes regarding the kinds of stories about the United States that drift around in other parts of the world. And American tales about other parts of the world may be even less accurate.

It is imperative in this process not only to discern when information is solid, but to look at evidence from all sides of the question. Those who emphasize the nearness of the End love to talk about rising crime statistics, catastrophic earthquakes and floods, wars and rumors of wars, imminent economic collapse, and declining morality. And it isn't hard to find solid evidence and endless anecdotes to back up the assertion that things are as bad as they can get.

Credibility is severely damaged, however, when we ignore solid evidence that points in other directions. Truth can afford to be fair in its use of evidence. While crime in the United States is certainly a major concern, it has dropped by more than half in the last five years in my own home town of New York City. Teen-age pregnancy has dropped by thirty percent nationwide in the same period. And while you can always find a dozen economists who think the economy is about to crash, Adventist speakers and writers have been crying economic "wolf" since 1982. The irony is that the last seventeen years have witnessed the greatest economic boom in the history of the human race. While the End of all things may be at hand, a balanced look at the evidence suggests sanctified caution in our use of current events. We damage the credibility of all End-time preaching when we use inaccurate information or are selective in our use of solid evidence.

But what if your information is unquestionably solid? What if there really is danger of major computer-based dislocations when the millennium comes around? What if the pope really does want to force everyone to keep Sunday? What if "Mary" really does think that final events are just around the corner? What if there really are asteroids out there that could end all life on this planet in a moment? What if? One still has to determine whether solid information is of any spiritual significance or not. It is all too easy to jump to conclusions about the significance of particular world events.

Adventism has been prone to the quick assumption that particular world events are portents of an immediate end to all things. The church as an organized body has never set any date for the Second Coming. Significant leaders and lay people, however, have often succumbed to the temptation to proclaim certain events as particularly significant from a prophetic perspective.[5] But we need to keep in mind that this record is an embarrassment to us today. When we put the credibility of God or of His church on the line for the sake of private speculation, it lowers the credibility of both in the eyes of thinking people in the world.

Just because a person or an institution intends to damage the cause of God, it doesn't mean that they can or that they will. The pope may say that he would like to develop unity with the Jewish, Islamic, and Buddhist communities, but it doesn't mean he *can* right now. President Clinton may have executive powers that would enable him to declare Sunday a national holiday, but it doesn't mean he *will*.

Just because events are taking a course that reminds us of a particular prophecy, that doesn't mean that this particular event is what that prophecy was pointing to. Just because Satan reveals his plans through some emissary like "Mary," doesn't mean that God will let him carry any of them out (Rev 17:17). Just because one man proclaims a New World

Order, it doesn't prevent a New World Disorder from being just around the corner. Just because awesome events like the sudden fall of communism occur, that doesn't mean that they are the product of some human conspiracy. Just because enough weapons of mass destruction are out there to do us all in, it doesn't mean that God will allow humanity to destroy itself before the time.

The Bible makes clear that God is in full control of world events, all world events, including the activities of Satan (2 Thess. 2:9-12; Rev. 17:17). God, and God alone, knows when these events will take place (Matt. 24:36; Acts 1:6-7). The pope can do nothing unless God allows it. Mary can do nothing unless God allows it. The Trilateral Commission can do nothing unless God allows it. The United States can do nothing unless God allows it.

So go on watching world events in the light of prophecy. I plan to do the same. But remember that Adventists are expected to stay sober as we approach the End (1 Thess 5:1-11)! And don't forget the big picture. Adventists have never taught that Jesus could come at any moment. We have always recognized that certain things must first take place.[6] The gospel must go to the whole world before the end comes. That means it will become the object of worldwide attention. The secular and political powers of the world will unite in opposition to that gospel. The religious powers of the world will somehow unite in opposition to that gospel. The people of God will be thrust out of their ordinary ways of life and come under unusual stress.[7] While events are such that all the above could happen in a remarkably short time, the time factor remains hidden from us, and will remain so.

"We are not to live upon time excitement. . . . **no one will be able to predict** just when that time will come. . . . You **will not** be able to say that He will come **in one, two, or five years**, neither are you to put off his coming by stating that it may not be **for ten or twenty years**" (*Selected Messages*, book 1, p. 189).

1. Cloud et al, p. 70.
2. Ella Mae Rydzewski, "The Demons Among Us," *Adventist Review*, August 21, 1997, p. 6.
3. *The Great Controversy*, p. 371.

4. See Bauckham, pp. 306-310 for a discussion of the interpretive options and their proponents.

5. *What the Bible Says About the End-Time*, pp. 20-24.

6. This is a fundamental difference of perspective between Adventists and dispensationalists like Darby and Lindsey. See Kyle, p. 76.

7. For a more detailed analysis of the prophetic picture of final events and their implications for current events, see *What the Bible Says About the End-Time*, pp. 139-152.

CHAPTER

7

Be Ye Therefore Ready: The "How To"

When Adventists think about the End, we tend to do so more with the head than with the heart. We find it much easier to discuss current events in general than our own personal hopes and fears. We find it easier to expound on details of prophecy and history than to have a living relationship with God. We find it much easier to speculate on the nature and timing of the events of the End time than to give people a practical path toward readiness for those events.

I would be remiss, therefore, if I did not conclude with some practical advice for Adventists facing the year 2000. What does it mean to get ready for Jesus' return? How can I get ready in the midst of the rough and tumble busyness of the Information Age? But before we talk about how to get ready, let me explore some dead ends along the path to readiness. In my experience with Adventist audiences on six continents, I have learned that there are four unhealthy ways that Adventists approach the issue of getting ready for Jesus' return.

OVERPLAYING THE NEARNESS OF THE END

The first type of unhealthy approach to the End, as we have seen, is a tendency to overplay the nearness of the End, to set dates and seek to build people's excitement about the absolute nearness of End-time events. And, as we have seen (chapter 5), it is not necessary to set an exact date in order to "hype" the End. General statements such as "this is the final generation," or "somewhere before the year 2000," or "shortly after the Jubilee" are vegetarian versions of date setting, but they can be just as distracting from genuine readiness as the real thing. And one day, someone will set a date that seems near, but turns out to be too far in the future and causes many to rest in false security until it is too late.[1]

What we desperately need is the clarity and certainty of His soon coming without the time factor. The coming of Jesus is truly near for all of us, even if He does not come within our lifetime. My Uncle Gunther died in the blessed hope just a couple of months ago. He died driving home after a Thanksgiving get-together, in the full confidence that he would live to see Jesus come. But in terms of his awareness and experience the coming of Jesus was even sooner than he expected. You see, from a Seventh-day Adventist perspective, unconsciousness in death means that the next thing a believer experiences after death is the coming of Jesus!

So even hyping the nearness of the End just isn't soon enough for those who die suddenly. The final events will take some time, anywhere from a few months to a couple of years. But many of us will not live that long. We need to be ready now, for none of us knows if our lives will finish out the day. A student once approached a rabbi and asked, "When should I get right with God?" The rabbi answered, "The day before you die." The student responded, "But when am I going to die?" The rabbi replied, "No one knows, therefore the Scriptures say, 'Today, if you will hear His voice, harden not your hearts.'" Overplaying the End is not a healthy way to be ready for Jesus' return. Not only that, it is the major culprit in the second unhealthy way that Adventists tend to approach the issue of getting ready for Jesus' return.

IGNORING THE END

The rejection of datesetting and speculation about the End has its own darker side. As people become disgusted with the excesses of "true believers" there is the strong temptation to swing the pendulum to its opposite extreme and give up all interest in final events and often even in Christian faith itself.

Many Adventists today are fed up with teaching and preaching about the End. They don't want to hear sermons or seminars on the subject. They say, "We have heard that the End is near for forty years, over and over, on and on, and nothing has happened. I'm sick of hearing about it." Others are sickened by events like those that happened in Waco, Texas. Christians who have derived energy from a constant anticipation of the End eventually grow weary. When the End does not come and time moves on, people become more and more cynical about discussions of the End, and lethargy is the result.

Worse yet, more and more Adventist thinkers, in settings where they feel safe enough to be totally candid, are willing to raise the question of whether or not there will ever be a second coming. The ongoing delay (from our perspective) has finally raised, even among Adventists, the figurative cry, "Where is this 'coming' he promised? Ever since our fathers died, everything goes on as it has since the beginning of creation." (2 Pet 3:4)

Many other Adventists still believe in the reality of Jesus' coming, but just want to hear about practical Christianity and living for Jesus in today's world. These are very important themes, but in themselves they do not constitute the full witness of Scripture. The Bible is full of teaching about the second coming of Jesus. Nearly a quarter of the New Testament is concerned with events related to the Second Coming in one form or another. No matter how painful it may be for some to talk about the End, ignoring the End is not an option for New Testament Christians. The New Testament is truly an Adventist book. This approach to readiness for Jesus' return will certainly not achieve the goal.

But what of those who have begun to doubt that there will ever be a literal coming of Jesus along with a literal end to history? They are not the first Christians to doubt, Paul faced a similar issue in Corinth. His answer then is no less relevant today.

> But if it is preached that Christ has been raised from the dead,
>> how can some of you say that there is no resurrection
>> of the dead?
> If there is no resurrection of the dead,
>> Then not even Christ has been raised.
> And if Christ has not been raised,

> our preaching is useless
> and so is your faith. . . .
> **If only for this life we have hope in Christ,**
> **we are to be pitied more than all men.**
> **But Christ has indeed been raised from the dead,**
> **the firstfruits of those who have fallen asleep. . . .**
> For as in Adam all die,
> so in Christ all will be made alive.
> **But each in his own turn:**
> **Christ, the firstfruits;**
> **then, when he comes,**
> **those who belong to him**
> 1 Cor. 15:12-14, 19-20, 22-23.

In this text Paul takes direct issue with those who would argue for both a "spiritualized" resurrection and second coming of Jesus, or even for the absence of that blessed hope. If we claim to be Adventists, yet doubt the reality of the Second Coming, Paul argues that our faith and our preaching are useless (1 Cor. 15:12-14). We are even worse off than pagans and atheists, who have tasted nothing better than this life and therefore hope for nothing better. According to Paul, to have tasted the gospel without hope of Jesus' return is to be in a most pitiable condition. To preach the reality of the Second Coming is not to preach some pie in the sky by and by. Belief in a real and literal second coming has a profound impact on the way we live today.[2] To deny the reality of the Second Coming is to give up the essence of what it means to be an Adventist.

For Paul the reality of the Second Coming is not grounded in calculations of its nearness, or in evidence from recent events. For Paul the reality of the Second Coming is grounded in the reality of the resurrection of Jesus. If Jesus was raised from the dead back in A.D. 31, our own resurrection at the return of Jesus is guaranteed. To doubt the Second Coming is to doubt the resurrection of Jesus. And if Jesus is not raised from the dead, then the gospel is an empty promise of good things.

It is understandable that the passage of time, and repeated speculations regarding the timing of the End, might cause many to question whether the coming of Jesus is truly near. But we must never allow our discouragement over the timing of the End to undermine our faith in the reality of the End. The gospel and the Second Coming should be distinguished as two acts of God, but they should never be separated in terms of reality. If the one is real, so is the other.

SHAMING TO THE END

Another unhealthy way that many Adventists approach the issue of getting ready for Jesus' return is to try and figure out who is to blame for the delay of the End. People read statements that suggest that "Christ would have come ere this" if His people had only been ready,[3] or "Christ is waiting with longing desire for the manifestation of Himself in His church."[4] They sometimes take the next step and seek to identify who is unready so they can shame them into action.

"If only those young people would stop bringing all that rock music into the worship service, then Jesus would come." "If only people would keep the Sabbath the way they used to, Jesus would come." "If only people would discover the true teaching about the human nature of Christ, the world would listen and Jesus could come." Many find it necessary to graphically and repeatedly portray the sins in the church and the world that might delay the Lord's return. They seem to believe that by thundering against the sins of the church they can shame many to wake up and take their Christian duties more seriously.

The Bible, on the other hand, teaches that God is in control of events at the End (2 Thess. 2:11; Rev. 17:17). He is fully qualified to reform the church or discipline it as needed (Rev. 3:19). The visible separation between faithful and unfaithful takes place only at the End, the Second Coming (Matt. 13:37-43; cf. 13:47-50; 25:31-33). We should not expect to attain an absolutely pure, *visible* body of believers on this earth before then. Until the Second Coming, believers may have a certain level of discernment, but only God will be fully able to judge. Until then there will always be cases in which believers must leave the judgment up to God.

The problem is that shame and blame theology doesn't work. It feels good but accomplishes little. It doesn't get anybody ready to meet Jesus. Those who dwell continually on their own shortcomings tend to get worse rather than better. On the other hand, those who focus on the sins of others find it easy to live in comfortable denial of their own shortcomings. When we spend our time examining the faults of others, we lose sight of the One who appears at the End.

> The closer you come to Jesus, the more faulty you will appear in your own eyes; for your vision will be clearer, and your imperfections will be seen in broad and distinct contrast to his perfect nature. This is evidence that Satan's delusions have lost their power; that the vivifying influence of the Spirit of God is arousing you.
>
> No deep-seated love for Jesus can dwell in the heart that does not realize its own sinfulness. The soul that is transformed by the grace of Christ will admire his divine character; but if we do not see our own moral deformity, it is unmistakable evidence that we have not had a view of the beauty and excellence of Christ (*Steps to Christ*, pp. 64, 65).

The closer you come to Jesus, the more clearly you see the defects in your own character, and the less inclined you become to blame the delay of the Advent on the shortcomings of others. There is a better way to promote readiness for the End.

FEARING THE END

Perhaps the most common unhealthy approach to getting ready for Jesus' return is fear. Many Adventists worry about the persecution and martyrdom that the Bible and the Spirit of Prophecy seem to predict for the final days of earth's history. Just the other day a ten-year-old girl said to me, "I used to want Jesus to come back real soon, but now I don't want Him to come back soon, because I'm afraid of the things that will happen before He comes."

Where did she learn that? I know she didn't get that at home. Did she learn about it from her friends? In church school? In Sabbath School? Does it really matter? Let's face it, reading the Book of Revelation and the book *The Great Controversy* can be scary business. Hiding in the mountains to escape prison, torture, and death is no one's idea of fun. Life is better for most people when the action and the adventure happen to someone else. No one wants to be hunted and despised. No one wants to be rejected by friends and family. No one wants to be imprisoned and tortured. Only the suicidal want to die.

Is it possible to face the End without fear? Is there a healthy approach to the more frightening events that lie just ahead of us? A helpful starting point is to remember the message of 1 Cor. 10:13:

> No temptation has seized you
> > except what is common to man.
> > And God is faithful;
> > he will not let you be tempted
> > **beyond what you can bear.**
> > But when you are tempted,
> > he will also provide a way out
> > so that you can stand up under it.

The message of this text needs to be burned into Adventist hearts. If you can't handle the events of the End, God won't ask you to go through them. Ellen White goes so far as to say that God will lay some people to rest before the End time because He knows they couldn't handle what is coming.[5] God is in control of the events of the End. If you commit yourself to Him, He will see you through. God knows what you can take and what you can't. You are safe trusting in Him.

I have another idea about the End that not everyone will agree with, but I base it on the history of some of the martyrs from the past. Servetus was condemned by Calvin to be burned at the stake for his heretic teachings. Now I don't agree with what Calvin did, but the part of the story that interests me here is that Servetus screamed in pain for thirty minutes as he burned. By way of contrast, the godly reformer Huss sang hymns throughout his burning, right up to his last breath. He apparently never felt the flames.

What I get from this is that among the spiritual gifts there seems to be a gift of martyrdom. It is a gift that you can only exercise once! But if God should decide to allow you to witness for Him unto death, there is nothing to fear in the ultimate sense. You will not receive more than you can bear. God will be with you and give you whatever it takes to make it through. If God should choose you to be one of His ultimate heroes, He will give you all the courage and all the pain control that you will need.

On the positive side of End-time persecution we need to remember that Jesus is worth whatever we have to go through to get to Him. The time of trouble is nothing more than a passageway to Jesus.

I remember a video I saw a long time ago called *The Princess Bride.* In the story a young man falls in love with a princess, but he is captured by the Dread Pirate Roberts. She is kidnapped and moved far away. The young man follows. He crosses a passage in a rough sea. Then he climbs a thousand-foot-high cliff by rope. Then he faces the world's best swordsman. After defeating him he must face a giant hurling boulders at him and then engaging him in a wrestling match. After defeating the giant he outsmarts a genius who tries to trick him into drinking poison. He then tumbles down a steep hill, passes through a valley where fire belches up out of the ground, takes on Rodents of Unusual Size, and is finally captured and tortured nearly to death.

Unable to walk and barely able to move, he must now engineer the storming of a heavily defended castle with a force of only three men (including the swordsman and the giant who have come over onto his side). After desperate battle he finally gains his bride. And at the end of the video it is clear from the look on his face that it was worth it all in order to be with her.

So it is with the troubles of the End time. Surely what you may have to go through in the time of trouble will not be much worse than what that young man went through to attain his bride. And the prize will be all the greater, for Jesus is the greatest person you could ever know or ever want to know. If you know Him, the troubles of the End time will be a short interruption on your way to Him. It will be worth going through because at the End you will see Him face to face and carrying on a living, breathing, talking, listening and doing relationship with Him. When you attain eternity, the troubles of the End time will appear as nothing by way of contrast.

HOW TO GET READY

Now that we have looked at some unhealthy approaches to readiness for the coming of Jesus, we come to the matter that transcends all others as we approach the End. We have noticed earlier that the End is about Jesus more than it is about events or ideas. The following text is illustrative.

Now this is eternal life,
> that they might know you,
> the only true God,
> and Jesus Christ
> whom you have sent.
>> John 17:3.

In his message to the last-day church, Laodicea, Jesus says,

Here I am!
> I stand at the door and knock.
> If anyone hears my voice
> and opens the door,
> I will come in
> and eat with him,
> and he with me.
>> Rev. 3:20

The tragedy of the lost at the End is not the quality of their theology, or the lack of good deeds; rather Jesus laments, "I never knew you." (Matt. 7:21-23; 25:12) The climax of the End time is not the battle of Armageddon, but the "glorious appearing of our great God and Savior; Jesus Christ." (Titus 2:13)

Ellen White emphatically agrees that knowing Jesus is the key factor in a healthy approach to the End. Notice the following statement which was quoted in part in chapter 5:

The shortness of time is urged as an incentive for us to seek righteousness and to make Christ our friend. This is not the great motive. It savors of selfishness. Is it necessary that the terrors of the day of God be held before us to compel us through fear to right action? This ought not to be. *Jesus is attractive.* He is full of love, mercy, and compassion. *He proposes to be our friend,* to walk with us through all the rough pathways of life. He says to you, I am the Lord thy God; walk with me, and I will fill thy path with light. Jesus, the Majesty of Heaven, proposes *to elevate to companionship with himself those who come to him* with their burdens, their weaknesses, and their cares. *He will make them his dear children*, and finally give them an inheritance of more value than the empires of kings, a crown of glory richer than has ever decked the brow of the most exalted earthly monarch (*Review and Herald*, August 2, 1881, p. 89).

What a beautiful summary of the centrality of a relationship with Jesus in a healthy anticipation of the End! It is the daily walk, the daily companionship that sets the stage for our expectation of an eternity with the same person!

And who is Jesus after all? Why would anyone wait for Him? Why would anyone want to be in relationship with Him? Because He is far greater than any sports figure, greater than any movie star, greater than any earthly ruler. Jesus is the ruler of the entire universe. Bill Clinton and other earthly rulers have enough trouble ruling themselves. To know Jesus is to know the greatest there is. He made everything there is, everything worth having or talking about. He is the ultimate superstar.

But better than this, He knows all about you. Very few people who admire Michael Jordan, Leonardo DiCaprio or Nelson Mandela have ever met them, much less become known by them. But the King of the universe knows all about you, everything you have ever done, thought, or said. "Uh, Oh," you are saying to yourself right now, "I'm in really big trouble!" That's just it. Not only does Jesus know all about you, He loves you just the way you are. No matter what you have done, what you have said, or where you have gone, you are infinitely precious to Him.

A beautiful thing about this is that your relationship with Jesus doesn't require secrets. There is nothing He could find out about you that he doesn't already know. You needn't worry that He will come up with something you did a long time ago, or even something you're thinking right now, and say, "Oh, if that's the way you are, I won't have anything more to do with you!" There is no reason to fear confessing the truth about yourself to Him. He already knows! Nothing you could reveal about yourself could cause Him to leave you or change His mind about you. Your relationship with Him is secure as long as you are willing.

But best of all, He lives forever. He will never abandon you through death. Your relationship with Him is totally secure. These four special qualities (the King of the universe, who knows all about you, yet loves you just the same, and will never die) make Jesus the greatest possible companion any human being could have. A relationship with Him is worth more than any movie star, more than the whole world, more than the universe, more than life itself. A living relationship with Jesus is so precious that thousands have willingly gone to their deaths rather than renounce their relationship with Jesus.

HOW TO KNOW JESUS

The concept of a living and vibrant relationship with Jesus, however, raises a problem. How do you have that kind of relationship with Him? How do you get so close to Him that you know that you are ready for whatever the End time could bring? How do you get so close to Jesus that the Second Coming becomes your longing desire? How do you overcome the greatest obstacle to a relationship with Jesus? What obstacle? The obstacle of distance. How do you have a relationship with someone you cannot see, hear or touch? How do you have a relationship with someone who is not physically there?

As I write these lines we have just come through the great craze over the movie *Titanic. Titanic* earned twice as much money from theater admissions as any other movie of all time. What was the reason for this "titanic" excitement? One major factor was the apocalyptic interests of the director, James Cameron. An avid student of biblical apocalyptic (an earlier movie unabashedly copied the basic plot of the book of Revelation), he turned a movie about an 85-year-old disaster into a parable of our times. In the sinking ship many in the audience sensed a prophetic pronouncement about the fragility of human technology and even the future of the human race itself.

But there was another, more trivial, reason for the popularity of the film. Millions of teenage girls in North America became smitten with the handsome young male lead, Leonardo DiCaprio. Many went back to see the movie several times, some claim to have seen it over forty times! They were developing a relationship with someone they couldn't see, hear, or touch! Few of them have ever seen him in person.

But wait a minute! Couldn't they see and hear him in the movies he has made? Yes, in a sense. But the movies are not Leonardo. The movies are only a *witness* to the reality that is Leonardo. How do you know Leonardo DiCaprio even exists if you've never met him, heard him, or touched him? You have millions of people testifying to his existence. You hear about him on radio or TV, you read about him in magazines and newspapers. No one doubts his existence, even though few have met him.

The existence of Jesus is even more secure. Where millions will testify to the existence of Leonardo DiCaprio and the influence he may have had in their lives, *billions* over the centuries have testified to the existence of Jesus, including the testimonies found in the sacred and inspired pages of Scripture. The current craze over Leonardo DiCaprio testifies how you can have a real relationship with someone you cannot see, hear or touch. You develop that relationship by *spending time* with the *witness* about that person. You read about him, you listen to others who know him, you sample his own testimony about himself on TV, radio, or in a magazine. And for many young women in today's world, their relationship with Leonardo is the most significant thing that has ever happened to them, even though they have never met him in person.

So it is with Jesus. If you want to have a living and vital relationship with Him, you need to spend time with the witness about Him in His Word. You need to invest serious time in Bible study. You need to talk to other people who know Him, and hear their testimonies about His impact in their lives. You need to get involved in the mission that He left for His disciples (Matt. 28:20) to accomplish.

Can you imagine what it would be like for a young woman, who has spent weeks of her life getting to know Leonardo through film, TV, and magazines, to suddenly have the opportunity to meet him in person? Or to become his companion? To know him and be known by him? Would she be willing to pass through all kinds of difficulties in order to be with him? Of course she would.

Yet Leonardo is nothing compared with Jesus. Jesus is the King of the whole universe; Leonardo has enough trouble ruling his own emotions. Jesus knows all about you; Leonardo could care less whether you or I exist. Jesus loves you as you are, Leonardo cares only about a small circle of family and friends. And Jesus will be looking great throughout eternity. Will Leonardo look nearly as cute when he is 87 (I'm trying to get a point across to young people here; I'm not trying to offend octogenarians)? A relationship with Jesus is the greatest thing a person could ever pursue.

Around eight years ago I taught a couple of classes at Helderberg College in South Africa. I spent five whole weeks away from my wife for the first time. It was not an easy experience. What do you think? As the "delay" in our relationship grew longer and longer did I begin to forget her? Did I get tired of waiting and begin setting imaginary dates for my return? No! I spent those five weeks thinking about her more than I had ever thought of her before. In fact she was never sweeter, never more beautiful to me than she was during that period of absence. The longer the time went the more eagerly I antici-pated our eventual reunion. I "tasted" our relationship over and over in my mind's eye, and my longing for her grew and grew.

So it is with the return of Jesus. He is worth all the time and energy we could possibly expend in getting to know Him. He is worth going through all the troubles of the End time and then some. He is worth at least a thoughtful hour every day, reviewing His character in our minds' eye. As our relationship with Him is renewed every day, our desire to be closer grows. Getting face to face with Jesus is what anticipation of the End is all about. And when our attention is constantly fixed on Him no amount of delay will spoil our eager-ness to see, hear, and touch Him.

So what is the bottom line for today? If you are spending more time with Leonardo DiCaprio than you are with Jesus, you have made an important choice in terms of your priorities. And I can assure that Leonardo will not be there for you when the End time comes! If you are spending more time with *Titanic* and other media productions, or in listening to secular music, than you are with your Bible, Jesus cannot be the all-in-all priority that you need Him to be in your life. Getting to know Jesus means spending time with the great Witness about Him in Scripture. It means talking to other people who know Him, and hearing their testimonies about their own relationship with Him. It means getting involved in His mission to the world.

As we approach the End time, life confronts us with two great witnesses to individuals with whom one can have a real relationship even though at a distance. These witnesses are the Bible and the movie *Titanic*. Which is worth more investment of your time? *Titanic* may be a real attention-grabber, but one day it will be forgotten. The Bible, on the other hand, will always be there. The male lead of *Titanic* can never compare with Jesus. Jesus is the Greatest. So the choice is really a simple one. Remember, the Word of God will last forever. *Titanic*, on the other hand, is going down!

---

1. Ellen G. White, *The Great Controversy*, p. 457.
2. See chapter seven of my book *What the Bible Says About the End-Time* for an elaboration of the powerful impact that the reality of the Second Coming has on everyday life and ethics.
3. Ellen G. White, *Evangelism*, pp. 695-696.
4. Idem, *Christ's Object Lessons*, p. 69.
5. Idem, *Counsels on Health*, p. 375.